GUANGDONG PROVINCE (

PART 7

中国广东省地址集

LEARN SIMPLE CHINESE CHARACTERS, WORDS, SENTENCES, AND PHRASES

外国人学汉语

English Pinyin & Simplified Mandarin Chinese Character Edition, Suitable for Foreigners of HSK All Levels

Qiaqia Wu 吴恰恰

ACKNOWLEDGEMENT

This work wouldn't have been possible without the support of my friends, colleagues, and family members. I would like to express my deepest gratitude to my friends, teachers, colleagues, and loved ones to help me reach this milestone to produce books to help the foreigners better understand the Chinese addresses, language, and culture.

Thank you!

INTRODUCTION

This book is for the foreigners to learn simple Chinese sentences. To make the sentences relevant for you to better understanding of Mandarin Chinese, I have selected sentences based on the locations in the mainland China. By understanding these sentences, you will be able to understand and appreciate Chinese locations better. For example, knowledge of these locations will help you use the Chinese navigation Apps (Baidu, Gaode) conveniently. Here is an example sentence-

Example sentence in Chinese (location):

广东省广州市花都区翰智公寓 26 栋 46 层 7 室（邮政编码：441914）

Example sentence in pinyin:

Guǎngdōng Shěng Guǎngzhōu Shì Huā Dū Qū Hàn Zhì Gōngyù 26 Dòng 46 Céng 7 Shì （Yóuzhèng Biānmǎ：441914）

Example sentence in English:

Room# 7, Floor# 46, Building# 26, Han Zhi Apartment, Huadu District, Guangzhou City, Guangdong Province.

CONTENTS

CHAPTER 1: SENTENCES (1-20)

1201。博物院

广东省肇庆市鼎湖区克金路 380 号肇庆博物馆（邮政编码：202147）。联系电话：30754561。电子邮箱：zrsog@hcznglmv.museums.cn

Guǎngdōng Shěng Zhàoqìng Shì Dǐng Hú Qū Kè Jīn Lù 380 Hào Zàoqng Bó Wù Guǎn （Yóuzhèng Biānmǎ：202147). Liánxì Diànhuà：30754561. Diànzǐ Yóuxiāng：zrsog@hcznglmv.museums.cn

Zhaoqing Museum, 380 Ke Jin Road, Dinghu District, Zhaoqing, Guangdong. Postal Code: 202147. Phone Number：30754561. E-mail：zrsog@hcznglmv.museums.cn

1202。大学

广东省茂名市茂南区源光大学维胜路 974 号（邮政编码：419615）。联系电话：75426386。电子邮箱：vrsuy@ivpajdhe.edu.cn

Guǎngdōng Shěng Màomíng Shì Mào Nán Qū Yuán Guāng DàxuéWéi Shēng Lù 974 Hào （Yóuzhèng Biānmǎ：419615). Liánxì Diànhuà：75426386. Diànzǐ Yóuxiāng：vrsuy@ivpajdhe.edu.cn

Yuan Guang University, 974 Wei Sheng Road, Maonan District, Maoming, Guangdong. Postal Code: 419615. Phone Number：75426386. E-mail：vrsuy@ivpajdhe.edu.cn

1203。广场

广东省中山市寰彬路 703 号南顺广场（邮政编码：861835）。联系电话：60338091。电子邮箱：ybrmu@azorfguk.squares.cn

Guǎngdōng Shěng Zhōngshān Shì Huán Bīn Lù 703 Hào Nán Shùn Guǎng Chǎng (Yóuzhèng Biānmǎ：861835). Liánxì Diànhuà：60338091. Diànzǐ Yóuxiāng：ybrmu@azorfguk.squares.cn

Nan Shun Square, 703 Huan Bin Road, Zhongshan, Guangdong. Postal Code: 861835. Phone Number：60338091. E-mail：ybrmu@azorfguk.squares.cn

1204。医院

广东省深圳市南山区焯陶路 627 号乙队医院（邮政编码：804982）。联系电话：75070034。电子邮箱：meofj@kwgzyavp.health.cn

Guǎngdōng Shěng Shēnzhèn Shì Nánshānqū Chāo Táo Lù 627 Hào Yǐ Duì Yī Yuàn (Yóuzhèng Biānmǎ：804982). Liánxì Diànhuà：75070034. Diànzǐ Yóuxiāng：meofj@kwgzyavp.health.cn

Yi Dui Hospital, 627 Chao Tao Road, Nanshan District, Shenzhen, Guangdong. Postal Code: 804982. Phone Number：75070034. E-mail：meofj@kwgzyavp.health.cn

1205。公司

广东省佛山市三水区成原路 601 号阳跃有限公司（邮政编码：357325）。联系电话：82510195。电子邮箱：vbjhp@oudapcmh.biz.cn

Guǎngdōng Shěng Fúshān Shì Sān Shuǐ Qū Chéng Yuán Lù 601 Hào Yáng Yuè Yǒuxiàn Gōngsī (Yóuzhèng Biānmǎ：357325). Liánxì Diànhuà：82510195. Diànzǐ Yóuxiāng：vbjhp@oudapcmh.biz.cn

Yang Yue Corporation, 601 Cheng Yuan Road, Sanshui District, Foshan, Guangdong. Postal Code: 357325. Phone Number：82510195. E-mail：vbjhp@oudapcmh.biz.cn

1206。大学

广东省中山市晗游大学员继路 852 号（邮政编码：718104）。联系电话：66236986。电子邮箱：cpeho@gbmovwec.edu.cn

Guǎngdōng Shěng Zhōngshān Shì Hán Yóu DàxuéYún Jì Lù 852 Hào（Yóuzhèng Biānmǎ：718104). Liánxì Diànhuà：66236986. Diànzǐ Yóuxiāng：cpeho@gbmovwec.edu.cn

Han You University, 852 Yun Ji Road, Zhongshan, Guangdong. Postal Code: 718104. Phone Number：66236986. E-mail：cpeho@gbmovwec.edu.cn

1207。公司

广东省东莞市渊翰路 453 号帆际有限公司（ 邮政编码：193895）。联系电话：30499877。电子邮箱：sfoct@uijlhztc.biz.cn

Guǎngdōng Shěng Dōngguǎn Shì Yuān Hàn Lù 453 Hào Fān Jì Yǒuxiàn Gōngsī (Yóuzhèng Biānmǎ：193895). Liánxì Diànhuà：30499877. Diànzǐ Yóuxiāng：sfoct@uijlhztc.biz.cn

Fan Ji Corporation, 453 Yuan Han Road, Dongguan, Guangdong. Postal Code: 193895. Phone Number：30499877. E-mail：sfoct@uijlhztc.biz.cn

1208。公司

广东省揭阳市普宁市珂胜路 485 号勇阳有限公司（ 邮政编码：992255）。联系电话：16759969。电子邮箱：icfas@jtseqpum.biz.cn

Guǎngdōng Shěng Jiēyáng Shì Pǔníng Shì Kē Shēng Lù 485 Hào Yǒng Yáng Yǒuxiàn Gōngsī (Yóuzhèng Biānmǎ：992255). Liánxì Diànhuà：16759969. Diànzǐ Yóuxiāng：icfas@jtseqpum.biz.cn

Yong Yang Corporation, 485 Ke Sheng Road, Puning City, Jieyang, Guangdong. Postal Code: 992255. Phone Number：16759969. E-mail：icfas@jtseqpum.biz.cn

1209。医院

广东省珠海市金湾区臻食路 779 号大坡医院（ 邮政编码：311443）。联系电话：94908243。电子邮箱：pzsht@frdhtsui.health.cn

Guǎngdōng Shěng Zhūhǎi Shì Jīn Wān Qū Zhēn Sì Lù 779 Hào Dà Pō Yī Yuàn (Yóuzhèng Biānmǎ：311443). Liánxì Diànhuà：94908243. Diànzǐ Yóuxiāng：pzsht@frdhtsui.health.cn

Da Po Hospital, 779 Zhen Si Road, Jinwan District, Zhuhai, Guangdong. Postal Code: 311443. Phone Number：94908243. E-mail：pzsht@frdhtsui.health.cn

1210。医院

广东省惠州市惠城区焯恩路 920 号智迅医院（邮政编码：318882）。联系电话：73666205。电子邮箱：tuajm@xscmuqvw.health.cn

Guǎngdōng Shěng Huìzhōu Shì Huì Chéngqū Zhuō Ēn Lù 920 Hào Zhì Xùn Yī Yuàn (Yóuzhèng Biānmǎ：318882). Liánxì Diànhuà：73666205. Diànzǐ Yóuxiāng：tuajm@xscmuqvw.health.cn

Zhi Xun Hospital, 920 Zhuo En Road, Huicheng District, Huizhou, Guangdong. Postal Code: 318882. Phone Number：73666205. E-mail：tuajm@xscmuqvw.health.cn

1211。广场

广东省江门市台山市珏黎路 841 号来强广场（邮政编码：894189）。联系电话：42079255。电子邮箱：vjure@pgzoteja.squares.cn

Guǎngdōng Shěng Jiāngmén Shì Táishān Shì Jué Lí Lù 841 Hào Lái Qiǎng Guǎng Chǎng (Yóuzhèng Biānmǎ：894189). Liánxì Diànhuà：42079255. Diànzǐ Yóuxiāng：vjure@pgzoteja.squares.cn

Lai Qiang Square, 841 Jue Li Road, Taishan City, Jiangmen, Guangdong. Postal Code: 894189. Phone Number：42079255. E-mail：vjure@pgzoteja.squares.cn

1212。公司

广东省江门市新会区其中路 857 号波绅有限公司（邮政编码：874474）。联系电话：98896766。电子邮箱：mdilw@sxfyoiml.biz.cn

Guǎngdōng Shěng Jiāngmén Shì Xīn Huì Qū Qí Zhōng Lù 857 Hào Bō Shēn Yǒuxiàn Gōngsī (Yóuzhèng Biānmǎ：874474). Liánxì Diànhuà：98896766. Diànzǐ Yóuxiāng：mdilw@sxfyoiml.biz.cn

Bo Shen Corporation, 857 Qi Zhong Road, Xinhui District, Jiangmen, Guangdong. Postal Code: 874474. Phone Number：98896766. E-mail：mdilw@sxfyoiml.biz.cn

1213。大学

广东省梅州市丰顺县辙尚大学继兵路 798 号（邮政编码：489891）。联系电话：40964936。电子邮箱：gpwac@wdmepbrt.edu.cn

Guǎngdōng Shěng Méizhōu Shì Fēng Shùn Xiàn Zhé Shàng DàxuéJì Bīng Lù 798 Hào (Yóuzhèng Biānmǎ：489891). Liánxì Diànhuà：40964936. Diànzǐ Yóuxiāng：gpwac@wdmepbrt.edu.cn

Zhe Shang University, 798 Ji Bing Road, Fengshun County, Meizhou, Guangdong. Postal Code: 489891. Phone Number：40964936. E-mail：gpwac@wdmepbrt.edu.cn

1214。公共汽车站

广东省阳江市阳东区龙中路 476 号沛振站（邮政编码：696158）。联系电话：70693301。电子邮箱：gpewy@fhpkyanb.transport.cn

Guǎngdōng Shěng Yángjiāng Shì Yáng Dōngqū Lóng Zhōng Lù 476 Hào Bèi Zhèn Zhàn (Yóuzhèng Biānmǎ：696158). Liánxì Diànhuà：70693301. Diànzǐ Yóuxiāng：gpewy@fhpkyanb.transport.cn

Bei Zhen Bus Station, 476 Long Zhong Road, Yangdong District, Yangjiang, Guangdong. Postal Code: 696158. Phone Number：70693301. E-mail：gpewy@fhpkyanb.transport.cn

1215。寺庙

广东省江门市鹤山市克发路 782 号俊福寺（ 邮政编码：749637）。联系电话：83483219。电子邮箱：ndypj@qtzgosmd.god.cn

Guǎngdōng Shěng Jiāngmén Shì Hèshān Shì Kè Fā Lù 782 Hào Jùn Fú Sì (Yóuzhèng Biānmǎ：749637). Liánxì Diànhuà：83483219. Diànzǐ Yóuxiāng：ndypj@qtzgosmd.god.cn

Jun Fu Temple, 782 Ke Fa Road, Heshan City, Jiangmen, Guangdong. Postal Code: 749637. Phone Number：83483219. E-mail：ndypj@qtzgosmd.god.cn

1216。大学

广东省汕头市金平区山轶大学冠渊路 307 号（ 邮政编码：615573）。联系电话：34448904。电子邮箱：gmkar@vredmotj.edu.cn

Guǎngdōng Shěng Shàntóu Shì Jīnpíng Qū Shān Yì DàxuéGuān Yuān Lù 307 Hào (Yóuzhèng Biānmǎ：615573). Liánxì Diànhuà：34448904. Diànzǐ Yóuxiāng：gmkar@vredmotj.edu.cn

Shan Yi University, 307 Guan Yuan Road, Jinping District, Shantou, Guangdong. Postal Code: 615573. Phone Number：34448904. E-mail：gmkar@vredmotj.edu.cn

1217。公司

广东省汕头市龙湖区盛冠路 326 号炯庆有限公司（ 邮政编码：323749）。联系电话：83377271。电子邮箱：loftg@vbnuezrd.biz.cn

Guǎngdōng Shěng Shàntóu Shì Lónghúqū Shèng Guàn Lù 326 Hào Jiǒng Qìng Yǒuxiàn Gōngsī (Yóuzhèng Biānmǎ：323749). Liánxì Diànhuà：83377271. Diànzǐ Yóuxiāng：loftg@vbnuezrd.biz.cn

Jiong Qing Corporation, 326 Sheng Guan Road, Longhu District, Shantou, Guangdong. Postal Code: 323749. Phone Number：83377271. E-mail：loftg@vbnuezrd.biz.cn

<h2>1218。公司</h2>

广东省河源市和平县食龙路 262 号不辉有限公司（邮政编码：414673）。联系电话：53903396。电子邮箱：frbgl@gitulone.biz.cn

Guǎngdōng Shěng Héyuán Shì Hépíng Xiàn Yì Lóng Lù 262 Hào Bù Huī Yǒuxiàn Gōngsī (Yóuzhèng Biānmǎ：414673). Liánxì Diànhuà：53903396. Diànzǐ Yóuxiāng：frbgl@gitulone.biz.cn

Bu Hui Corporation, 262 Yi Long Road, Heping County, Heyuan, Guangdong. Postal Code: 414673. Phone Number：53903396. E-mail：frbgl@gitulone.biz.cn

<h2>1219。寺庙</h2>

广东省中山市际学路 789 号冕白寺（邮政编码：592719）。联系电话：57255865。电子邮箱：wziyh@cvmapejr.god.cn

Guǎngdōng Shěng Zhōngshān Shì Jì Xué Lù 789 Hào Miǎn Bái Sì (Yóuzhèng Biānmǎ：592719). Liánxì Diànhuà：57255865. Diànzǐ Yóuxiāng：wziyh@cvmapejr.god.cn

Mian Bai Temple, 789 Ji Xue Road, Zhongshan, Guangdong. Postal Code: 592719. Phone Number：57255865. E-mail：wziyh@cvmapejr.god.cn

<h2>1220。医院</h2>

广东省湛江市麻章区中黎路 215 号迅舟医院（邮政编码：544859）。联系电话：56963024。电子邮箱：atguy@yxeuhcow.health.cn

Guǎngdōng Shěng Zhànjiāng Shì Má Zhāng Qū Zhōng Lí Lù 215 Hào Xùn Zhōu Yī Yuàn (Yóuzhèng Biānmǎ：544859). Liánxì Diànhuà：56963024. Diànzǐ Yóuxiāng：atguy@yxeuhcow.health.cn

Xun Zhou Hospital, 215 Zhong Li Road, Machang District, Zhanjiang, Guangdong. Postal Code: 544859. Phone Number：56963024. E-mail：atguy@yxeuhcow.health.cn

CHAPTER 2: SENTENCES (21-40)

1221。公司

广东省肇庆市四会市先陶路 453 号俊坚有限公司（邮政编码：807945）。联系电话：98990888。电子邮箱：kxpnq@weiyhklq.biz.cn

Guǎngdōng Shěng Zhàoqìng Shì Sì Huì Shì Xiān Táo Lù 453 Hào Jùn Jiān Yǒuxiàn Gōngsī (Yóuzhèng Biānmǎ：807945). Liánxì Diànhuà：98990888. Diànzǐ Yóuxiāng：kxpnq@weiyhklq.biz.cn

Jun Jian Corporation, 453 Xian Tao Road, Sihui City, Zhaoqing, Guangdong. Postal Code: 807945. Phone Number：98990888. E-mail：kxpnq@weiyhklq.biz.cn

1222。广场

广东省韶关市新丰县际圣路 994 号员进广场（邮政编码：988323）。联系电话：45062787。电子邮箱：xlfyo@zvgxeons.squares.cn

Guǎngdōng Shěng Sháoguān Shì Xīn Fēngxiàn Jì Shèng Lù 994 Hào Yuán Jìn Guǎng Chǎng (Yóuzhèng Biānmǎ：988323). Liánxì Diànhuà：45062787. Diànzǐ Yóuxiāng：xlfyo@zvgxeons.squares.cn

Yuan Jin Square, 994 Ji Sheng Road, Xinfeng County, Shaoguan, Guangdong. Postal Code: 988323. Phone Number：45062787. E-mail：xlfyo@zvgxeons.squares.cn

1223。酒店

广东省阳江市阳春市食恩路 561 号郁启酒店（邮政编码：697398）。联系电话：16259948。电子邮箱：zuyjr@iqspwlay.biz.cn

Guǎngdōng Shěng Yángjiāng Shì Yángchūn Shì Sì Ēn Lù 561 Hào Yù Qǐ Jiǔ Diàn (Yóuzhèng Biānmǎ：697398). Liánxì Diànhuà：16259948. Diànzǐ Yóuxiāng：zuyjr@iqspwlay.biz.cn

Yu Qi Hotel, 561 Si En Road, Yangchun City, Yangjiang, Guangdong. Postal Code: 697398. Phone Number：16259948. E-mail：zuyjr@iqspwlay.biz.cn

1224。公司

广东省肇庆市四会市钊威路 466 号领可有限公司（邮政编码：717706）。联系电话：70765308。电子邮箱：aifnq@wdigyuzt.biz.cn

Guǎngdōng Shěng Zhàoqìng Shì Sì Huì Shì Zhāo Wēi Lù 466 Hào Lǐng Kě Yǒuxiàn Gōngsī (Yóuzhèng Biānmǎ：717706). Liánxì Diànhuà：70765308. Diànzǐ Yóuxiāng：aifnq@wdigyuzt.biz.cn

Ling Ke Corporation, 466 Zhao Wei Road, Sihui City, Zhaoqing, Guangdong. Postal Code: 717706. Phone Number：70765308. E-mail：aifnq@wdigyuzt.biz.cn

1225。火车站

广东省肇庆市高要区咚山路 216 号肇庆站（邮政编码：767235）。联系电话：18743486。电子邮箱：voekh@jaeovsqf.chr.cn

Guǎngdōng Shěng Zhàoqìng Shì Gāo Yào Qū Dōng Shān Lù 216 Hào Zàoqng Zhàn (Yóuzhèng Biānmǎ：767235). Liánxì Diànhuà：18743486. Diànzǐ Yóuxiāng：voekh@jaeovsqf.chr.cn

Zhaoqing Railway Station, 216 Dong Shan Road, Gaoyao District, Zhaoqing, Guangdong. Postal Code: 767235. Phone Number：18743486. E-mail：voekh@jaeovsqf.chr.cn

1226。公园

广东省韶关市乳源瑶族自治县翰波路 708 号白其公园（邮政编码：465692）。联系电话：20082074。电子邮箱：ipfco@xgpfhrvt.parks.cn

Guǎngdōng Shěng Sháoguān Shì Rǔ Yuán Yáozú Zìzhìxiàn Hàn Bō Lù 708 Hào Bái Qí Gōng Yuán (Yóuzhèng Biānmǎ：465692). Liánxì Diànhuà：20082074. Diànzǐ Yóuxiāng：ipfco@xgpfhrvt.parks.cn

Bai Qi Park, 708 Han Bo Road, Ruyuan Yao Autonomous County, Shaoguan, Guangdong. Postal Code: 465692. Phone Number：20082074. E-mail：ipfco@xgpfhrvt.parks.cn

1227。医院

广东省阳江市阳西县译桥路 280 号毅洵医院（邮政编码：759302）。联系电话：47235737。电子邮箱：cpkhy@okzcmbjl.health.cn

Guǎngdōng Shěng Yángjiāng Shì Yáng Xī Xiàn Yì Qiáo Lù 280 Hào Yì Xún Yī Yuàn (Yóuzhèng Biānmǎ：759302). Liánxì Diànhuà：47235737. Diànzǐ Yóuxiāng：cpkhy@okzcmbjl.health.cn

Yi Xun Hospital, 280 Yi Qiao Road, Yangxi County, Yangjiang, Guangdong. Postal Code: 759302. Phone Number：47235737. E-mail：cpkhy@okzcmbjl.health.cn

1228。寺庙

广东省江门市鹤山市坡禹路 293 号惟食寺（邮政编码：284173）。联系电话：24043292。电子邮箱：ohcdn@icngrovp.god.cn

Guǎngdōng Shěng Jiāngmén Shì Hèshān Shì Pō Yǔ Lù 293 Hào Wéi Yì Sì (Yóuzhèng Biānmǎ：284173). Liánxì Diànhuà：24043292. Diànzǐ Yóuxiāng：ohcdn@icngrovp.god.cn

Wei Yi Temple, 293 Po Yu Road, Heshan City, Jiangmen, Guangdong. Postal Code: 284173. Phone Number：24043292. E-mail：ohcdn@icngrovp.god.cn

1229。火车站

广东省佛山市三水区可山路 590 号佛山站（邮政编码：212340）。联系电话：66178738。电子邮箱：mwzfg@eugbknlx.chr.cn

Guǎngdōng Shěng Fúshān Shì Sān Shuǐ Qū Kě Shān Lù 590 Hào Fúsān Zhàn (Yóuzhèng Biānmǎ：212340). Liánxì Diànhuà：66178738. Diànzǐ Yóuxiāng：mwzfg@eugbknlx.chr.cn

Foshan Railway Station, 590 Ke Shan Road, Sanshui District, Foshan, Guangdong. Postal Code: 212340. Phone Number：66178738. E-mail：mwzfg@eugbknlx.chr.cn

1230。大学

广东省惠州市龙门县楚发大学隆圣路 786 号（邮政编码：540295）。联系电话：66047890。电子邮箱：akrmx@ihdouezp.edu.cn

Guǎngdōng Shěng Huìzhōu Shì Lóngmén Xiàn Chǔ Fā DàxuéLóng Shèng Lù 786 Hào（Yóuzhèng Biānmǎ：540295). Liánxì Diànhuà：66047890. Diànzǐ Yóuxiāng：akrmx@ihdouezp.edu.cn

Chu Fa University, 786 Long Sheng Road, Longmen County, Huizhou, Guangdong. Postal Code: 540295. Phone Number：66047890. E-mail：akrmx@ihdouezp.edu.cn

1231。火车站

广东省阳江市阳东区茂白路 719 号阳江站（邮政编码：447097）。联系电话：39887585。电子邮箱：jcywm@nqlotyxi.chr.cn

Guǎngdōng Shěng Yángjiāng Shì Yáng Dōngqū Mào Bái Lù 719 Hào Yángjiāng Zhàn（Yóuzhèng Biānmǎ：447097). Liánxì Diànhuà：39887585. Diànzǐ Yóuxiāng：jcywm@nqlotyxi.chr.cn

Yangjiang Railway Station, 719 Mao Bai Road, Yangdong District, Yangjiang, Guangdong. Postal Code: 447097. Phone Number：39887585. E-mail：jcywm@nqlotyxi.chr.cn

1232。广场

广东省惠州市惠东县威来路 651 号顺晗广场（邮政编码：927582）。联系电话：72957259。电子邮箱：idmfw@izdqnohy.squares.cn

Guǎngdōng Shěng Huìzhōu Shì Huì Dōng Xiàn Wēi Lái Lù 651 Hào Shùn Hán Guǎng Chǎng（Yóuzhèng Biānmǎ：927582). Liánxì Diànhuà：72957259. Diànzǐ Yóuxiāng：idmfw@izdqnohy.squares.cn

Shun Han Square, 651 Wei Lai Road, Huidong County, Huizhou, Guangdong. Postal Code: 927582. Phone Number：72957259. E-mail：idmfw@izdqnohy.squares.cn

1233。酒店

广东省韶关市始兴县豹世路 685 号学星酒店（邮政编码：598524）。联系电话：60310872。电子邮箱：oejzm@chfpisvz.biz.cn

Guǎngdōng Shěng Sháoguān Shì Shǐ Xìng Xiàn Bào Shì Lù 685 Hào Xué Xīng Jiǔ Diàn（Yóuzhèng Biānmǎ：598524). Liánxì Diànhuà：60310872. Diànzǐ Yóuxiāng：oejzm@chfpisvz.biz.cn

Xue Xing Hotel, 685 Bao Shi Road, Shixing County, Shaoguan, Guangdong. Postal Code: 598524. Phone Number：60310872. E-mail：oejzm@chfpisvz.biz.cn

1234。公共汽车站

广东省汕头市潮阳区晗院路 804 号轶波站（邮政编码：287207）。联系电话：99715015。电子邮箱：diuwn@tmrbeyxg.transport.cn

Guǎngdōng Shěng Shàntóu Shì Cháoyáng Qū Hán Yuàn Lù 804 Hào Yì Bō Zhàn（Yóuzhèng Biānmǎ：287207). Liánxì Diànhuà：99715015. Diànzǐ Yóuxiāng：diuwn@tmrbeyxg.transport.cn

Yi Bo Bus Station, 804 Han Yuan Road, Chaoyang District, Shantou, Guangdong. Postal Code: 287207. Phone Number：99715015. E-mail：diuwn@tmrbeyxg.transport.cn

1235。湖泊

广东省清远市佛冈县渊冠路 856 号食友湖（邮政编码：428734）。联系电话：77602204。电子邮箱：fhyls@ilvngfkc.lakes.cn

Guǎngdōng Shěng Qīngyuǎn Shì Fú Gāng Xiàn Yuān Guān Lù 856 Hào Yì Yǒu Hú (Yóuzhèng Biānmǎ：428734). Liánxì Diànhuà：77602204. Diànzǐ Yóuxiāng：fhyls@ilvngfkc.lakes.cn

Yi You Lake, 856 Yuan Guan Road, Fogang County, Qingyuan, Guangdong. Postal Code: 428734. Phone Number：77602204. E-mail：fhyls@ilvngfkc.lakes.cn

1236。广场

广东省汕头市龙湖区守食路 624 号继智广场（邮政编码：343659）。联系电话：54019277。电子邮箱：vaymc@tufxpksh.squares.cn

Guǎngdōng Shěng Shàntóu Shì Lónghúqū Shǒu Yì Lù 624 Hào Jì Zhì Guǎng Chǎng (Yóuzhèng Biānmǎ：343659). Liánxì Diànhuà：54019277. Diànzǐ Yóuxiāng：vaymc@tufxpksh.squares.cn

Ji Zhi Square, 624 Shou Yi Road, Longhu District, Shantou, Guangdong. Postal Code: 343659. Phone Number：54019277. E-mail：vaymc@tufxpksh.squares.cn

1237。公园

广东省茂名市化州市科谢路 186 号翰威公园（邮政编码：754581）。联系电话：78491222。电子邮箱：ejgvo@vkcsnzly.parks.cn

Guǎngdōng Shěng Màomíng Shì Huà Zhōu Shì Kē Xiè Lù 186 Hào Hàn Wēi Gōng Yuán（Yóuzhèng Biānmǎ：754581). Liánxì Diànhuà：78491222. Diànzǐ Yóuxiāng：ejgvo@vkcsnzly.parks.cn

Han Wei Park, 186 Ke Xie Road, Huazhou, Maoming, Guangdong. Postal Code: 754581. Phone Number：78491222. E-mail：ejgvo@vkcsnzly.parks.cn

1238。家庭

广东省湛江市徐闻县寰维路 428 号绅岐公寓 30 层 201 室（邮政编码：636033）。联系电话：79807052。电子邮箱：szcbx@yqzdoxvc.cn

Guǎngdōng Shěng Zhànjiāng Shì Xúwén Xiàn Huán Wéi Lù 428 Hào Shēn Qí Gōng Yù 30 Céng 201 Shì (Yóuzhèng Biānmǎ：636033). Liánxì Diànhuà：79807052. Diànzǐ Yóuxiāng：szcbx@yqzdoxvc.cn

Room# 201, Floor# 30, Shen Qi Apartment, 428 Huan Wei Road, Xuwen County, Zhanjiang, Guangdong. Postal Code: 636033. Phone Number：79807052. E-mail：szcbx@yqzdoxvc.cn

1239。大学

广东省肇庆市鼎湖区食鹤大学秀晖路 337 号（邮政编码：345084）。联系电话：13553688。电子邮箱：bhqag@ahqpzdbk.edu.cn

Guǎngdōng Shěng Zhàoqìng Shì Dǐng Hú Qū Shí Hè DàxuéXiù Huī Lù 337 Hào (Yóuzhèng Biānmǎ：345084). Liánxì Diànhuà：13553688. Diànzǐ Yóuxiāng：bhqag@ahqpzdbk.edu.cn

Shi He University, 337 Xiu Hui Road, Dinghu District, Zhaoqing, Guangdong. Postal Code: 345084. Phone Number：13553688. E-mail：bhqag@ahqpzdbk.edu.cn

1240。寺庙

广东省佛山市顺德区兆阳路 685 号中员寺（邮政编码：243533）。联系电话：41489513。电子邮箱：dpjba@svyqabpl.god.cn

Guǎngdōng Shěng Fúshān Shì Shùndé Qū Zhào Yáng Lù 685 Hào Zhòng Yuán Sì (Yóuzhèng Biānmǎ：243533). Liánxì Diànhuà：41489513. Diànzǐ Yóuxiāng：dpjba@svyqabpl.god.cn

Zhong Yuan Temple, 685 Zhao Yang Road, Shunde, Foshan, Guangdong. Postal Code: 243533. Phone Number：41489513. E-mail：dpjba@svyqabpl.god.cn

CHAPTER 3: SENTENCES (41-60)

1241。医院

广东省中山市食员路 617 号国冠医院（邮政编码：699369）。联系电话：84008971。电子邮箱：xmjqu@yhjwtapq.health.cn

Guǎngdōng Shěng Zhōngshān Shì Sì Yuán Lù 617 Hào Guó Guān Yī Yuàn (Yóuzhèng Biānmǎ：699369). Liánxì Diànhuà：84008971. Diànzǐ Yóuxiāng：xmjqu@yhjwtapq.health.cn

Guo Guan Hospital, 617 Si Yuan Road, Zhongshan, Guangdong. Postal Code: 699369. Phone Number：84008971. E-mail：xmjqu@yhjwtapq.health.cn

1242。公司

广东省江门市蓬江区彬亭路 341 号宝来有限公司（邮政编码：216370）。联系电话：45098772。电子邮箱：quisw@rcdemqzi.biz.cn

Guǎngdōng Shěng Jiāngmén Shì Péng Jiāng Qū Bīn Tíng Lù 341 Hào Bǎo Lái Yǒuxiàn Gōngsī (Yóuzhèng Biānmǎ：216370). Liánxì Diànhuà：45098772. Diànzǐ Yóuxiāng：quisw@rcdemqzi.biz.cn

Bao Lai Corporation, 341 Bin Ting Road, Pengjiang District, Jiangmen, Guangdong. Postal Code: 216370. Phone Number：45098772. E-mail：quisw@rcdemqzi.biz.cn

1243。家庭

广东省惠州市博罗县仓钊路 804 号继臻公寓 28 层 255 室（邮政编码：933938）。联系电话：50965745。电子邮箱：dozkc@ducfwikz.cn

Guǎngdōng Shěng Huìzhōu Shì Bó Luō Xiàn Cāng Zhāo Lù 804 Hào Jì Zhēn Gōng Yù 28 Céng 255 Shì (Yóuzhèng Biānmǎ：933938). Liánxì Diànhuà：50965745. Diànzǐ Yóuxiāng：dozkc@ducfwikz.cn

Room# 255, Floor# 28, Ji Zhen Apartment, 804 Cang Zhao Road, Boluo County, Huizhou, Guangdong. Postal Code: 933938. Phone Number：50965745. E-mail：dozkc@ducfwikz.cn

1244。火车站

广东省阳江市江城区土德路 547 号阳江站（ 邮政编码：724249）。联系电话：94997944。电子邮箱：iwber@rdenbuvq.chr.cn

Guǎngdōng Shěng Yángjiāng Shì Jiāng Chéngqū Tǔ Dé Lù 547 Hào Yángjiāng Zhàn (Yóuzhèng Biānmǎ：724249). Liánxì Diànhuà：94997944. Diànzǐ Yóuxiāng：iwber@rdenbuvq.chr.cn

Yangjiang Railway Station, 547 Tu De Road, Jiangcheng District, Yangjiang, Guangdong. Postal Code: 724249. Phone Number：94997944. E-mail：iwber@rdenbuvq.chr.cn

1245。博物院

广东省梅州市梅江区亮自路 543 号梅州博物馆（ 邮政编码：745514）。联系电话：54064638。电子邮箱：qkinj@zvyqubrt.museums.cn

Guǎngdōng Shěng Méizhōu Shì Méi Jiāng Qū Liàng Zì Lù 543 Hào Méizōu Bó Wù Guǎn (Yóuzhèng Biānmǎ：745514). Liánxì Diànhuà：54064638. Diànzǐ Yóuxiāng：qkinj@zvyqubrt.museums.cn

Meizhou Museum, 543 Liang Zi Road, Meijiang District, Meizhou, Guangdong. Postal Code: 745514. Phone Number：54064638. E-mail：qkinj@zvyqubrt.museums.cn

1246。大学

广东省广州市天河区学白大学嘉立路 684 号（ 邮政编码：950548）。联系电话：65033436。电子邮箱：kareq@iztuakgx.edu.cn

Guǎngdōng Shěng Guǎngzhōu Shì Tiānhé Qū Xué Bái DàxuéJiā Lì Lù 684 Hào (Yóuzhèng Biānmǎ：950548). Liánxì Diànhuà：65033436. Diànzǐ Yóuxiāng：kareq@iztuakgx.edu.cn

Xue Bai University, 684 Jia Li Road, Tianhe District, Guangzhou, Guangdong. Postal Code: 950548. Phone Number：65033436. E-mail：kareq@iztuakgx.edu.cn

1247。湖泊

广东省阳江市阳西县员祥路 837 号水独湖（邮政编码：412627）。联系电话：52636032。电子邮箱：kvyic@wpcnqbkl.lakes.cn

Guǎngdōng Shěng Yángjiāng Shì Yáng Xī Xiàn Yún Xiáng Lù 837 Hào Shuǐ Dú Hú (Yóuzhèng Biānmǎ：412627). Liánxì Diànhuà：52636032. Diànzǐ Yóuxiāng：kvyic@wpcnqbkl.lakes.cn

Shui Du Lake, 837 Yun Xiang Road, Yangxi County, Yangjiang, Guangdong. Postal Code: 412627. Phone Number：52636032. E-mail：kvyic@wpcnqbkl.lakes.cn

1248。公司

广东省湛江市麻章区大宝路 318 号不不有限公司（邮政编码：846637）。联系电话：80486585。电子邮箱：pvuoh@yckabndu.biz.cn

Guǎngdōng Shěng Zhànjiāng Shì Má Zhāng Qū Dài Bǎo Lù 318 Hào Bù Bù Yǒuxiàn Gōngsī (Yóuzhèng Biānmǎ：846637). Liánxì Diànhuà：80486585. Diànzǐ Yóuxiāng：pvuoh@yckabndu.biz.cn

Bu Bu Corporation, 318 Dai Bao Road, Machang District, Zhanjiang, Guangdong. Postal Code: 846637. Phone Number：80486585. E-mail：pvuoh@yckabndu.biz.cn

1249。公司

广东省汕头市潮南区兵学路 614 号九游有限公司（邮政编码：149601）。联系电话：51540591。电子邮箱：krgcq@xpzogtbl.biz.cn

Guǎngdōng Shěng Shàntóu Shì Cháo Nán Qū Bīng Xué Lù 614 Hào Jiǔ Yóu Yǒuxiàn Gōngsī (Yóuzhèng Biānmǎ：149601). Liánxì Diànhuà：51540591. Diànzǐ Yóuxiāng：krgcq@xpzogtbl.biz.cn

Jiu You Corporation, 614 Bing Xue Road, Chaonan District, Shantou, Guangdong. Postal Code: 149601. Phone Number：51540591. E-mail：krgcq@xpzogtbl.biz.cn

1250。公共汽车站

广东省梅州市平远县俊谢路 387 号石化站（ 邮政编码：595912）。联系电话：96330843。电子邮箱：zmnuk@wsbcdutm.transport.cn

Guǎngdōng Shěng Méizhōu Shì Píng Yuǎn Xiàn Jùn Xiè Lù 387 Hào Shí Huà Zhàn (Yóuzhèng Biānmǎ：595912). Liánxì Diànhuà：96330843. Diànzǐ Yóuxiāng：zmnuk@wsbcdutm.transport.cn

Shi Hua Bus Station, 387 Jun Xie Road, Pingyuan County, Meizhou, Guangdong. Postal Code: 595912. Phone Number：96330843. E-mail：zmnuk@wsbcdutm.transport.cn

1251。火车站

广东省云浮市新兴县立食路 921 号云浮站（ 邮政编码：968735）。联系电话：80632540。电子邮箱：kqugh@pwgdaroy.chr.cn

Guǎngdōng Shěng Yúnfú Shì Xīnxīng Xiàn Lì Shí Lù 921 Hào Yúnfú Zhàn (Yóuzhèng Biānmǎ：968735). Liánxì Diànhuà：80632540. Diànzǐ Yóuxiāng：kqugh@pwgdaroy.chr.cn

Yunfu Railway Station, 921 Li Shi Road, Xinxing County, Yunfu, Guangdong. Postal Code: 968735. Phone Number：80632540. E-mail：kqugh@pwgdaroy.chr.cn

1252。公共汽车站

广东省江门市鹤山市原原路 150 号可计站（ 邮政编码：632160）。联系电话：49500036。电子邮箱：bjryp@tdmwrnau.transport.cn

Guǎngdōng Shěng Jiāngmén Shì Hèshān Shì Yuán Yuán Lù 150 Hào Kě Jì Zhàn (Yóuzhèng Biānmǎ：632160). Liánxì Diànhuà：49500036. Diànzǐ Yóuxiāng：bjryp@tdmwrnau.transport.cn

Ke Ji Bus Station, 150 Yuan Yuan Road, Heshan City, Jiangmen, Guangdong. Postal Code: 632160. Phone Number：49500036. E-mail：bjryp@tdmwrnau.transport.cn

1253。公司

广东省广州市花都区近食路 717 号毅斌有限公司（邮政编码：445928）。联系电话：41966320。电子邮箱：agzfm@iuxsveok.biz.cn

Guǎngdōng Shěng Guǎngzhōu Shì Huā Dū Qū Jìn Shí Lù 717 Hào Yì Bīn Yǒuxiàn Gōngsī (Yóuzhèng Biānmǎ：445928). Liánxì Diànhuà：41966320. Diànzǐ Yóuxiāng：agzfm@iuxsveok.biz.cn

Yi Bin Corporation, 717 Jin Shi Road, Huadu District, Guangzhou, Guangdong. Postal Code: 445928. Phone Number：41966320. E-mail：agzfm@iuxsveok.biz.cn

1254。博物院

广东省阳江市江城区磊食路 533 号阳江博物馆（邮政编码：642846）。联系电话：72357847。电子邮箱：mijlw@waojsnmu.museums.cn

Guǎngdōng Shěng Yángjiāng Shì Jiāng Chéngqū Lěi Shí Lù 533 Hào Yángjiāng Bó Wù Guǎn (Yóuzhèng Biānmǎ：642846). Liánxì Diànhuà：72357847. Diànzǐ Yóuxiāng：mijlw@waojsnmu.museums.cn

Yangjiang Museum, 533 Lei Shi Road, Jiangcheng District, Yangjiang, Guangdong. Postal Code: 642846. Phone Number：72357847. E-mail：mijlw@waojsnmu.museums.cn

1255。博物院

广东省佛山市顺德区刚易路 236 号佛山博物馆（邮政编码：210737）。联系电话：34828150。电子邮箱：ldvbq@vgompjac.museums.cn

Guǎngdōng Shěng Fúshān Shì Shùndé Qū Gāng Yì Lù 236 Hào Fúsān Bó Wù Guǎn (Yóuzhèng Biānmǎ：210737). Liánxì Diànhuà：34828150. Diànzǐ Yóuxiāng：ldvbq@vgompjac.museums.cn

Foshan Museum, 236 Gang Yi Road, Shunde, Foshan, Guangdong. Postal Code: 210737. Phone Number：34828150. E-mail：ldvbq@vgompjac.museums.cn

1256。公共汽车站

广东省云浮市云城区智黎路 851 号冕征站（邮政编码：775232）。联系电话：60045092。电子邮箱：hywbd@cwnjpikf.transport.cn

Guǎngdōng Shěng Yúnfú Shì Yún Chéngqū Zhì Lí Lù 851 Hào Miǎn Zhēng Zhàn (Yóuzhèng Biānmǎ：775232). Liánxì Diànhuà：60045092. Diànzǐ Yóuxiāng：hywbd@cwnjpikf.transport.cn

Mian Zheng Bus Station, 851 Zhi Li Road, Yuncheng District, Yunfu, Guangdong. Postal Code: 775232. Phone Number：60045092. E-mail：hywbd@cwnjpikf.transport.cn

1257。医院

广东省揭阳市揭西县翼圣路 465 号翰钢医院（邮政编码：600379）。联系电话：79384487。电子邮箱：gjhwo@xlvakztj.health.cn

Guǎngdōng Shěng Jiēyáng Shì Jiē Xī Xiàn Yì Shèng Lù 465 Hào Hàn Gāng Yī Yuàn (Yóuzhèng Biānmǎ：600379). Liánxì Diànhuà：79384487. Diànzǐ Yóuxiāng：gjhwo@xlvakztj.health.cn

Han Gang Hospital, 465 Yi Sheng Road, Jiexi County, Jieyang, Guangdong. Postal Code: 600379. Phone Number：79384487. E-mail：gjhwo@xlvakztj.health.cn

1258。大学

广东省韶关市翁源县鹤尚大学伦其路 405 号（邮政编码：975758）。联系电话：28759428。电子邮箱：keafm@naehzdwx.edu.cn

Guǎngdōng Shěng Sháoguān Shì Wēng Yuán Xiàn Hè Shàng DàxuéLún Qí Lù 405 Hào（Yóuzhèng Biānmǎ：975758). Liánxì Diànhuà：28759428. Diànzǐ Yóuxiāng：keafm@naehzdwx.edu.cn

He Shang University, 405 Lun Qi Road, Wengyuan County, Shaoguan, Guangdong. Postal Code: 975758. Phone Number：28759428. E-mail：keafm@naehzdwx.edu.cn

1259。大学

广东省云浮市新兴县征晗大学坡熔路 582 号（邮政编码：438158）。联系电话：37965696。电子邮箱：rthwq@hjowdizn.edu.cn

Guǎngdōng Shěng Yúnfú Shì Xīnxīng Xiàn Zhēng Hán DàxuéPō Róng Lù 582 Hào（Yóuzhèng Biānmǎ：438158). Liánxì Diànhuà：37965696. Diànzǐ Yóuxiāng：rthwq@hjowdizn.edu.cn

Zheng Han University, 582 Po Rong Road, Xinxing County, Yunfu, Guangdong. Postal Code: 438158. Phone Number：37965696. E-mail：rthwq@hjowdizn.edu.cn

1260。湖泊

广东省汕头市龙湖区澜帆路 441 号翼来湖（邮政编码：821795）。联系电话：83637906。电子邮箱：zmown@gfcebdjx.lakes.cn

Guǎngdōng Shěng Shàntóu Shì Lónghúqū Lán Fān Lù 441 Hào Yì Lái Hú（Yóuzhèng Biānmǎ：821795). Liánxì Diànhuà：83637906. Diànzǐ Yóuxiāng：zmown@gfcebdjx.lakes.cn

Yi Lai Lake, 441 Lan Fan Road, Longhu District, Shantou, Guangdong. Postal Code: 821795. Phone Number：83637906. E-mail：zmown@gfcebdjx.lakes.cn

CHAPTER 4: SENTENCES (61-80)

1261。火车站

广东省中山市坡铁路 555 号中山站（邮政编码：984163）。联系电话：21197072。电子邮箱：kdqia@uprqzxnc.chr.cn

Guǎngdōng Shěng Zhōngshān Shì Pō Fū Lù 555 Hào Zōngsān Zhàn（Yóuzhèng Biānmǎ：984163). Liánxì Diànhuà：21197072. Diànzǐ Yóuxiāng：kdqia@uprqzxnc.chr.cn

Zhongshan Railway Station, 555 Po Fu Road, Zhongshan, Guangdong. Postal Code: 984163. Phone Number：21197072. E-mail：kdqia@uprqzxnc.chr.cn

1262。公园

广东省珠海市香洲区九金路 177 号世其公园（邮政编码：875405）。联系电话：61644152。电子邮箱：lxudm@gzfdvnex.parks.cn

Guǎngdōng Shěng Zhūhǎi Shì Xiāngzhōu Qū Jiǔ Jīn Lù 177 Hào Shì Qí Gōng Yuán（Yóuzhèng Biānmǎ：875405). Liánxì Diànhuà：61644152. Diànzǐ Yóuxiāng：lxudm@gzfdvnex.parks.cn

Shi Qi Park, 177 Jiu Jin Road, Xiangzhou District, Zhuhai, Guangdong. Postal Code: 875405. Phone Number：61644152. E-mail：lxudm@gzfdvnex.parks.cn

1263。公园

广东省广州市越秀区熔晗路 484 号德豹公园（邮政编码：957551）。联系电话：93960598。电子邮箱：kfyal@xmybptoz.parks.cn

Guǎngdōng Shěng Guǎngzhōu Shì Yuèxiù Qū Róng Hán Lù 484 Hào Dé Bào Gōng Yuán（Yóuzhèng Biānmǎ：957551). Liánxì Diànhuà：93960598. Diànzǐ Yóuxiāng：kfyal@xmybptoz.parks.cn

De Bao Park, 484 Rong Han Road, Yuexiu District, Guangzhou, Guangdong. Postal Code: 957551. Phone Number：93960598. E-mail：kfyal@xmybptoz.parks.cn

1264。大学

广东省广州市荔湾区员绅大学王屹路 788 号（邮政编码：768971）。联系电话：22830717。电子邮箱：hbgdx@ndfwrtms.edu.cn

Guǎngdōng Shěng Guǎngzhōu Shì Lìwān Qū Yuán Shēn Dàxué Wàng Yì Lù 788 Hào (Yóuzhèng Biānmǎ：768971). Liánxì Diànhuà：22830717. Diànzǐ Yóuxiāng：hbgdx@ndfwrtms.edu.cn

Yuan Shen University, 788 Wang Yi Road, Liwan District, Guangzhou, Guangdong. Postal Code: 768971. Phone Number：22830717. E-mail：hbgdx@ndfwrtms.edu.cn

1265。大学

广东省茂名市信宜市庆俊大学福亮路 776 号（邮政编码：574513）。联系电话：68811521。电子邮箱：uheyp@roptjway.edu.cn

Guǎngdōng Shěng Màomíng Shì Xìn Yí Shì Qìng Jùn Dàxué Fú Liàng Lù 776 Hào (Yóuzhèng Biānmǎ：574513). Liánxì Diànhuà：68811521. Diànzǐ Yóuxiāng：uheyp@roptjway.edu.cn

Qing Jun University, 776 Fu Liang Road, Xinyi City, Maoming, Guangdong. Postal Code: 574513. Phone Number：68811521. E-mail：uheyp@roptjway.edu.cn

1266。酒店

广东省梅州市梅县区来陆路 405 号维世酒店（邮政编码：124573）。联系电话：59481688。电子邮箱：guhat@gyclaekq.biz.cn

Guǎngdōng Shěng Méizhōu Shì Méixiàn Qū Lái Liù Lù 405 Hào Wéi Shì Jiǔ Diàn (Yóuzhèng Biānmǎ：124573). Liánxì Diànhuà：59481688. Diànzǐ Yóuxiāng：guhat@gyclaekq.biz.cn

Wei Shi Hotel, 405 Lai Liu Road, Meixian District, Meizhou, Guangdong. Postal Code: 124573. Phone Number：59481688. E-mail：guhat@gyclaekq.biz.cn

1267。公园

广东省韶关市浈江区亚德路 323 号甫轶公园（邮政编码：621182）。联系电话：13884344。电子邮箱：zwxjb@tzmkxgbi.parks.cn

Guǎngdōng Shěng Sháoguān Shì Zhēn Jiāng Qū Yà Dé Lù 323 Hào Fǔ Yì Gōng Yuán (Yóuzhèng Biānmǎ：621182). Liánxì Diànhuà：13884344. Diànzǐ Yóuxiāng：zwxjb@tzmkxgbi.parks.cn

Fu Yi Park, 323 Ya De Road, Zhenjiang District, Shaoguan, Guangdong. Postal Code: 621182. Phone Number：13884344. E-mail：zwxjb@tzmkxgbi.parks.cn

1268。机场

广东省佛山市顺德区维冠路 328 号佛山福锡国际机场（邮政编码：119904）。联系电话：38233935。电子邮箱：gcfmn@uehnxyzs.airports.cn

Guǎngdōng Shěng Fúshān Shì Shùndé Qū Wéi Guàn Lù 328 Hào Fúsān Fú Xī Guó Jì Jī Chǎng (Yóuzhèng Biānmǎ：119904). Liánxì Diànhuà：38233935. Diànzǐ Yóuxiāng：gcfmn@uehnxyzs.airports.cn

Foshan Fu Xi International Airport, 328 Wei Guan Road, Shunde, Foshan, Guangdong. Postal Code: 119904. Phone Number：38233935. E-mail：gcfmn@uehnxyzs.airports.cn

1269。大学

广东省清远市清新区冠洵大学懂不路 842 号（邮政编码：765573）。联系电话：66637941。电子邮箱：nvazk@usbcpqfn.edu.cn

Guǎngdōng Shěng Qīngyuǎn Shì Qīngxīn Qū Guàn Xún DàxuéDǒng Bù Lù 842 Hào (Yóuzhèng Biānmǎ：765573). Liánxì Diànhuà：66637941. Diànzǐ Yóuxiāng：nvazk@usbcpqfn.edu.cn

Guan Xun University, 842 Dong Bu Road, Fresh Area, Qingyuan, Guangdong. Postal Code: 765573. Phone Number：66637941. E-mail：nvazk@usbcpqfn.edu.cn

1270。公共汽车站

广东省汕尾市城区绅成路 421 号冠盛站（邮政编码：691177）。联系电话：61228413。电子邮箱：ngvpi@fzaxgvqc.transport.cn

Guǎngdōng Shěng Shànwěi Shì Chéngqū Shēn Chéng Lù 421 Hào Guàn Shèng Zhàn (Yóuzhèng Biānmǎ：691177). Liánxì Diànhuà：61228413. Diànzǐ Yóuxiāng：ngvpi@fzaxgvqc.transport.cn

Guan Sheng Bus Station, 421 Shen Cheng Road, Urban Area, Shanwei, Guangdong. Postal Code: 691177. Phone Number：61228413. E-mail：ngvpi@fzaxgvqc.transport.cn

1271。湖泊

广东省河源市东源县轪其路 949 号腾桥湖（邮政编码：850503）。联系电话：65742361。电子邮箱：pntyx@flvdmqbu.lakes.cn

Guǎngdōng Shěng Héyuán Shì Dōng Yuán Xiàn Shì Qí Lù 949 Hào Téng Qiáo Hú (Yóuzhèng Biānmǎ：850503). Liánxì Diànhuà：65742361. Diànzǐ Yóuxiāng：pntyx@flvdmqbu.lakes.cn

Teng Qiao Lake, 949 Shi Qi Road, Dongyuan County, Heyuan, Guangdong. Postal Code: 850503. Phone Number：65742361. E-mail：pntyx@flvdmqbu.lakes.cn

1272。火车站

广东省湛江市遂溪县熔石路 531 号湛江站（邮政编码：170260）。联系电话：68294816。电子邮箱：yjnwg@euhzodbw.chr.cn

Guǎngdōng Shěng Zhànjiāng Shì Suì Xī Xiàn Róng Dàn Lù 531 Hào Zànjiāng Zhàn (Yóuzhèng Biānmǎ：170260). Liánxì Diànhuà：68294816. Diànzǐ Yóuxiāng：yjnwg@euhzodbw.chr.cn

Zhanjiang Railway Station, 531 Rong Dan Road, Suixi County, Zhanjiang, Guangdong. Postal Code: 170260. Phone Number：68294816. E-mail：yjnwg@euhzodbw.chr.cn

1273。医院

广东省清远市连州市不舟路 553 号独晖医院（邮政编码：691583）。联系电话：49259758。电子邮箱：ewrsg@cfwmbsay.health.cn

Guǎngdōng Shěng Qīngyuǎn Shì Lián Zhōu Shì Bù Zhōu Lù 553 Hào Dú Huī Yī Yuàn (Yóuzhèng Biānmǎ：691583). Liánxì Diànhuà：49259758. Diànzǐ Yóuxiāng：ewrsg@cfwmbsay.health.cn

Du Hui Hospital, 553 Bu Zhou Road, Lianzhou, Qingyuan, Guangdong. Postal Code: 691583. Phone Number：49259758. E-mail：ewrsg@cfwmbsay.health.cn

1274。广场

广东省茂名市电白区铁鸣路 516 号惟亚广场（邮政编码：815415）。联系电话：71372299。电子邮箱：txcma@degsjxrz.squares.cn

Guǎngdōng Shěng Màomíng Shì Diàn Bái Qū Fū Míng Lù 516 Hào Wéi Yà Guǎng Chǎng（Yóuzhèng Biānmǎ：815415). Liánxì Diànhuà：71372299. Diànzǐ Yóuxiāng：txcma@degsjxrz.squares.cn

Wei Ya Square, 516 Fu Ming Road, Dianbai District, Maoming, Guangdong. Postal Code: 815415. Phone Number：71372299. E-mail：txcma@degsjxrz.squares.cn

1275。博物院

广东省河源市龙川县乐盛路 994 号河源博物馆（邮政编码：439585）。联系电话：40920712。电子邮箱：zwlcn@aecypzts.museums.cn

Guǎngdōng Shěng Héyuán Shì Lóng Chuānxiàn Lè Shèng Lù 994 Hào Héyuán Bó Wù Guǎn (Yóuzhèng Biānmǎ：439585). Liánxì Diànhuà：40920712. Diànzǐ Yóuxiāng：zwlcn@aecypzts.museums.cn

Heyuan Museum, 994 Le Sheng Road, Longchuan County, Heyuan, Guangdong. Postal Code: 439585. Phone Number：40920712. E-mail：zwlcn@aecypzts.museums.cn

1276。家庭

广东省韶关市仁化县咚发路 851 号仲智公寓 38 层 915 室（邮政编码：401880）。联系电话：53431979。电子邮箱：tubxl@eahfxbmw.cn

Guǎngdōng Shěng Sháoguān Shì Rén Huà Xiàn Dōng Fā Lù 851 Hào Zhòng Zhì Gōng Yù 38 Céng 915 Shì (Yóuzhèng Biānmǎ：401880). Liánxì Diànhuà：53431979. Diànzǐ Yóuxiāng：tubxl@eahfxbmw.cn

Room# 915, Floor# 38, Zhong Zhi Apartment, 851 Dong Fa Road, Renhua County, Shaoguan, Guangdong. Postal Code: 401880. Phone Number：53431979. E-mail：tubxl@eahfxbmw.cn

1277。大学

广东省阳江市阳东区中先大学食恩路 841 号（邮政编码：150572）。联系电话：74706014。电子邮箱：aqohz@oaenvkui.edu.cn

Guǎngdōng Shěng Yángjiāng Shì Yáng Dōngqū Zhōng Xiān DàxuéSì Ēn Lù 841 Hào (Yóuzhèng Biānmǎ：150572). Liánxì Diànhuà：74706014. Diànzǐ Yóuxiāng：aqohz@oaenvkui.edu.cn

Zhong Xian University, 841 Si En Road, Yangdong District, Yangjiang, Guangdong. Postal Code: 150572. Phone Number：74706014. E-mail：aqohz@oaenvkui.edu.cn

1278。酒店

广东省珠海市斗门区南葆路 929 号世宽酒店（邮政编码：139557）。联系电话：63724484。电子邮箱：brgvq@moxszdbt.biz.cn

Guǎngdōng Shěng Zhūhǎi Shì Dòumén Qū Nán Bǎo Lù 929 Hào Shì Kuān Jiǔ Diàn (Yóuzhèng Biānmǎ：139557). Liánxì Diànhuà：63724484. Diànzǐ Yóuxiāng：brgvq@moxszdbt.biz.cn

Shi Kuan Hotel, 929 Nan Bao Road, Doumen District, Zhuhai, Guangdong. Postal Code: 139557. Phone Number：63724484. E-mail：brgvq@moxszdbt.biz.cn

1279。公共汽车站

广东省河源市源城区食咚路 841 号进熔站（邮政编码：171035）。联系电话：75935442。电子邮箱：qnrof@gcbztkyu.transport.cn

Guǎngdōng Shěng Héyuán Shì Yuán Chéngqū Shí Dōng Lù 841 Hào Jìn Róng Zhàn (Yóuzhèng Biānmǎ：171035). Liánxì Diànhuà：75935442. Diànzǐ Yóuxiāng：qnrof@gcbztkyu.transport.cn

Jin Rong Bus Station, 841 Shi Dong Road, Yuancheng District, Heyuan, Guangdong. Postal Code: 171035. Phone Number：75935442. E-mail：qnrof@gcbztkyu.transport.cn

1280。大学

广东省梅州市丰顺县克国大学维克路 800 号（邮政编码：512940）。联系电话：73632454。电子邮箱：kmlza@fdephsmi.edu.cn

Guǎngdōng Shěng Méizhōu Shì Fēng Shùn Xiàn Kè Guó DàxuéWéi Kè Lù 800 Hào (Yóuzhèng Biānmǎ：512940). Liánxì Diànhuà：73632454. Diànzǐ Yóuxiāng：kmlza@fdephsmi.edu.cn

Ke Guo University, 800 Wei Ke Road, Fengshun County, Meizhou, Guangdong. Postal Code: 512940. Phone Number：73632454. E-mail：kmlza@fdephsmi.edu.cn

CHAPTER 5: SENTENCES (81-100)

1281。公共汽车站

广东省韶关市乳源瑶族自治县石辙路 114 号员秀站（邮政编码：865038）。联系电话：60400146。电子邮箱：xbfue@kifayqhc.transport.cn

Guǎngdōng Shěng Sháoguān Shì Rǔ Yuán Yáozú Zìzhìxiàn Shí Zhé Lù 114 Hào Yuán Xiù Zhàn （Yóuzhèng Biānmǎ：865038). Liánxì Diànhuà：60400146. Diànzǐ Yóuxiāng：xbfue@kifayqhc.transport.cn

Yuan Xiu Bus Station, 114 Shi Zhe Road, Ruyuan Yao Autonomous County, Shaoguan, Guangdong. Postal Code: 865038. Phone Number：60400146. E-mail：xbfue@kifayqhc.transport.cn

1282。机场

广东省茂名市信宜市王自路 166 号茂名领亮国际机场（邮政编码：821348）。联系电话：95149833。电子邮箱：xyzeu@moerjqha.airports.cn

Guǎngdōng Shěng Màomíng Shì Xìn Yí Shì Wáng Zì Lù 166 Hào Màomíng Lǐng Liàng Guó Jì Jī Chǎng （Yóuzhèng Biānmǎ：821348). Liánxì Diànhuà：95149833. Diànzǐ Yóuxiāng：xyzeu@moerjqha.airports.cn

Maoming Ling Liang International Airport, 166 Wang Zi Road, Xinyi City, Maoming, Guangdong. Postal Code: 821348. Phone Number：95149833. E-mail：xyzeu@moerjqha.airports.cn

1283。寺庙

广东省肇庆市封开县院石路 395 号全星寺（邮政编码：145752）。联系电话：45166307。电子邮箱：kiyhj@dgrzijxc.god.cn

Guǎngdōng Shěng Zhàoqìng Shì Fēng Kāixiàn Yuàn Shí Lù 395 Hào Quán Xīng Sì (Yóuzhèng Biānmǎ：145752). Liánxì Diànhuà：45166307. Diànzǐ Yóuxiāng：kiyhj@dgrzijxc.god.cn

Quan Xing Temple, 395 Yuan Shi Road, Fengkai County, Zhaoqing, Guangdong. Postal Code: 145752. Phone Number：45166307. E-mail：kiyhj@dgrzijxc.god.cn

1284。火车站

广东省佛山市顺德区珏陆路 213 号佛山站（邮政编码：445560）。联系电话：43016551。电子邮箱：xmaft@hytvnlws.chr.cn

Guǎngdōng Shěng Fúshān Shì Shùndé Qū Jué Liù Lù 213 Hào Fúsān Zhàn (Yóuzhèng Biānmǎ：445560). Liánxì Diànhuà：43016551. Diànzǐ Yóuxiāng：xmaft@hytvnlws.chr.cn

Foshan Railway Station, 213 Jue Liu Road, Shunde, Foshan, Guangdong. Postal Code: 445560. Phone Number：43016551. E-mail：xmaft@hytvnlws.chr.cn

1285。广场

广东省汕头市金平区秀顺路 426 号金嘉广场（邮政编码：878540）。联系电话：71621677。电子邮箱：tmeun@iqcdgvxf.squares.cn

Guǎngdōng Shěng Shàntóu Shì Jīnpíng Qū Xiù Shùn Lù 426 Hào Jīn Jiā Guǎng Chǎng (Yóuzhèng Biānmǎ：878540). Liánxì Diànhuà：71621677. Diànzǐ Yóuxiāng：tmeun@iqcdgvxf.squares.cn

Jin Jia Square, 426 Xiu Shun Road, Jinping District, Shantou, Guangdong. Postal Code: 878540. Phone Number：71621677. E-mail：tmeun@iqcdgvxf.squares.cn

1286。酒店

广东省潮州市饶平县隆翼路 490 号独铁酒店（邮政编码：843111）。联系电话：74628406。电子邮箱：pyder@onpgjrqa.biz.cn

Guǎngdōng Shěng Cháozhōu Shì Ráo Píng Xiàn Lóng Yì Lù 490 Hào Dú Fū Jiǔ Diàn (Yóuzhèng Biānmǎ：843111). Liánxì Diànhuà：74628406. Diànzǐ Yóuxiāng：pyder@onpgjrqa.biz.cn

Du Fu Hotel, 490 Long Yi Road, Raoping County, Chaozhou, Guangdong. Postal Code: 843111. Phone Number：74628406. E-mail：pyder@onpgjrqa.biz.cn

1287。湖泊

广东省东莞市振超路 236 号亚帆湖 （邮政编码：154298）。联系电话：31463551。电子邮箱：zilby@xkntmgqb.lakes.cn

Guǎngdōng Shěng Dōngguǎn Shì Zhèn Chāo Lù 236 Hào Yà Fān Hú (Yóuzhèng Biānmǎ：154298). Liánxì Diànhuà：31463551. Diànzǐ Yóuxiāng：zilby@xkntmgqb.lakes.cn

Ya Fan Lake, 236 Zhen Chao Road, Dongguan, Guangdong. Postal Code: 154298. Phone Number：31463551. E-mail：zilby@xkntmgqb.lakes.cn

1288。酒店

广东省梅州市梅江区山楚路 117 号陆原酒店 （邮政编码：923616）。联系电话：69041451。电子邮箱：ipdcq@cpsukzrw.biz.cn

Guǎngdōng Shěng Méizhōu Shì Méi Jiāng Qū Shān Chǔ Lù 117 Hào Lù Yuán Jiǔ Diàn (Yóuzhèng Biānmǎ：923616). Liánxì Diànhuà：69041451. Diànzǐ Yóuxiāng：ipdcq@cpsukzrw.biz.cn

Lu Yuan Hotel, 117 Shan Chu Road, Meijiang District, Meizhou, Guangdong. Postal Code: 923616. Phone Number：69041451. E-mail：ipdcq@cpsukzrw.biz.cn

1289。公共汽车站

广东省茂名市化州市轶泽路 855 号译恩站 （邮政编码：569268）。联系电话：42243771。电子邮箱：pdbfa@hzcuyxra.transport.cn

Guǎngdōng Shěng Màomíng Shì Huà Zhōu Shì Shì Zé Lù 855 Hào Yì Ēn Zhàn (Yóuzhèng Biānmǎ：569268). Liánxì Diànhuà：42243771. Diànzǐ Yóuxiāng：pdbfa@hzcuyxra.transport.cn

Yi En Bus Station, 855 Shi Ze Road, Huazhou, Maoming, Guangdong. Postal Code: 569268. Phone Number：42243771. E-mail：pdbfa@hzcuyxra.transport.cn

1290。广场

广东省汕尾市海丰县九翰路 872 号化振广场（邮政编码：158629）。联系电话：57054682。电子邮箱：qfkpx@lhfszqbj.squares.cn

Guǎngdōng Shěng Shànwěi Shì Hǎi Fēngxiàn Jiǔ Hàn Lù 872 Hào Huà Zhèn Guǎng Chǎng（Yóuzhèng Biānmǎ：158629). Liánxì Diànhuà：57054682. Diànzǐ Yóuxiāng：qfkpx@lhfszqbj.squares.cn

Hua Zhen Square, 872 Jiu Han Road, Haifeng County, Shanwei, Guangdong. Postal Code: 158629. Phone Number：57054682. E-mail：qfkpx@lhfszqbj.squares.cn

1291。医院

广东省云浮市新兴县炯豪路 271 号谢洵医院（邮政编码：698851）。联系电话：55307769。电子邮箱：bzfyr@ipzxbjwk.health.cn

Guǎngdōng Shěng Yúnfú Shì Xīnxīng Xiàn Jiǒng Háo Lù 271 Hào Xiè Xún Yī Yuàn（Yóuzhèng Biānmǎ：698851). Liánxì Diànhuà：55307769. Diànzǐ Yóuxiāng：bzfyr@ipzxbjwk.health.cn

Xie Xun Hospital, 271 Jiong Hao Road, Xinxing County, Yunfu, Guangdong. Postal Code: 698851. Phone Number：55307769. E-mail：bzfyr@ipzxbjwk.health.cn

1292。公园

广东省惠州市龙门县近居路 536 号际领公园（邮政编码：275157）。联系电话：98673695。电子邮箱：mldsv@nvklbodq.parks.cn

Guǎngdōng Shěng Huìzhōu Shì Lóngmén Xiàn Jìn Jū Lù 536 Hào Jì Lǐng Gōng Yuán（Yóuzhèng Biānmǎ：275157). Liánxì Diànhuà：98673695. Diànzǐ Yóuxiāng：mldsv@nvklbodq.parks.cn

Ji Ling Park, 536 Jin Ju Road, Longmen County, Huizhou, Guangdong. Postal Code: 275157. Phone Number：98673695. E-mail：mldsv@nvklbodq.parks.cn

1293。湖泊

广东省佛山市三水区王帆路 962 号昌豪湖（ 邮政编码：374160）。联系电话：14604739。电子邮箱：nmhcl@vxfsyejp.lakes.cn

Guǎngdōng Shěng Fúshān Shì Sān Shuǐ Qū Wáng Fān Lù 962 Hào Chāng Háo Hú (Yóuzhèng Biānmǎ：374160). Liánxì Diànhuà：14604739. Diànzǐ Yóuxiāng：nmhcl@vxfsyejp.lakes.cn

Chang Hao Lake, 962 Wang Fan Road, Sanshui District, Foshan, Guangdong. Postal Code: 374160. Phone Number：14604739. E-mail：nmhcl@vxfsyejp.lakes.cn

1294。火车站

广东省湛江市雷州市来盛路 836 号湛江站（ 邮政编码：326630）。联系电话：75488713。电子邮箱：ychur@udoncsmi.chr.cn

Guǎngdōng Shěng Zhànjiāng Shì Léizhōu Shì Lái Shèng Lù 836 Hào Zànjiāng Zhàn (Yóuzhèng Biānmǎ：326630). Liánxì Diànhuà：75488713. Diànzǐ Yóuxiāng：ychur@udoncsmi.chr.cn

Zhanjiang Railway Station, 836 Lai Sheng Road, Leizhou, Zhanjiang, Guangdong. Postal Code: 326630. Phone Number：75488713. E-mail：ychur@udoncsmi.chr.cn

1295。机场

广东省河源市连平县兆秀路 846 号河源独可国际机场（ 邮政编码：840651）。联系电话：67145734。电子邮箱：zckhw@inzotabf.airports.cn

Guǎngdōng Shěng Héyuán Shì Lián Píng Xiàn Zhào Xiù Lù 846 Hào Héyuán Dú Kě Guó Jì Jī Chǎng (Yóuzhèng Biānmǎ：840651). Liánxì Diànhuà：67145734. Diànzǐ Yóuxiāng：zckhw@inzotabf.airports.cn

Heyuan Du Ke International Airport, 846 Zhao Xiu Road, Lianping County, Heyuan, Guangdong. Postal Code: 840651. Phone Number：67145734. E-mail：zckhw@inzotabf.airports.cn

1296。公共汽车站

广东省潮州市潮安区征进路 917 号白化站（ 邮政编码：396131）。联系电话：65504434。电子邮箱：ucdwr@phfmdiye.transport.cn

Guǎngdōng Shěng Cháozhōu Shì Cháo Ān Qū Zhēng Jìn Lù 917 Hào Bái Huā Zhàn (Yóuzhèng Biānmǎ：396131). Liánxì Diànhuà：65504434. Diànzǐ Yóuxiāng：ucdwr@phfmdiye.transport.cn

Bai Hua Bus Station, 917 Zheng Jin Road, Chaoan District, Chaozhou, Guangdong. Postal Code: 396131. Phone Number：65504434. E-mail：ucdwr@phfmdiye.transport.cn

1297。火车站

广东省茂名市茂南区龙辉路 991 号茂名站（ 邮政编码：258631）。联系电话：39440832。电子邮箱：mnqir@caxtiejm.chr.cn

Guǎngdōng Shěng Màomíng Shì Mào Nán Qū Lóng Huī Lù 991 Hào Màomíng Zhàn (Yóuzhèng Biānmǎ：258631). Liánxì Diànhuà：39440832. Diànzǐ Yóuxiāng：mnqir@caxtiejm.chr.cn

Maoming Railway Station, 991 Long Hui Road, Maonan District, Maoming, Guangdong. Postal Code: 258631. Phone Number：39440832. E-mail：mnqir@caxtiejm.chr.cn

1298。大学

广东省阳江市阳西县珂澜大学队澜路 883 号（ 邮政编码：445866）。联系电话：39950529。电子邮箱：fnmxg@elvauqth.edu.cn

Guǎngdōng Shěng Yángjiāng Shì Yáng Xī Xiàn Kē Lán DàxuéDuì Lán Lù 883 Hào (Yóuzhèng Biānmǎ: 445866). Liánxì Diànhuà: 39950529. Diànzǐ Yóuxiāng: fnmxg@elvauqth.edu.cn

Ke Lan University, 883 Dui Lan Road, Yangxi County, Yangjiang, Guangdong. Postal Code: 445866. Phone Number: 39950529. E-mail: fnmxg@elvauqth.edu.cn

1299。博物院

广东省阳江市阳西县宝成路 259 号阳江博物馆（邮政编码：452529）。联系电话：67867441。电子邮箱：vzqsg@zoukcfri.museums.cn

Guǎngdōng Shěng Yángjiāng Shì Yáng Xī Xiàn Bǎo Chéng Lù 259 Hào Yángjiāng Bó Wù Guǎn (Yóuzhèng Biānmǎ: 452529). Liánxì Diànhuà: 67867441. Diànzǐ Yóuxiāng: vzqsg@zoukcfri.museums.cn

Yangjiang Museum, 259 Bao Cheng Road, Yangxi County, Yangjiang, Guangdong. Postal Code: 452529. Phone Number: 67867441. E-mail: vzqsg@zoukcfri.museums.cn

1300。公园

广东省佛山市三水区浩桥路 732 号惟继公园（邮政编码：121759）。联系电话：49940002。电子邮箱：lkuyb@qmnhjvxp.parks.cn

Guǎngdōng Shěng Fúshān Shì Sān Shuǐ Qū Hào Qiáo Lù 732 Hào Wéi Jì Gōng Yuán (Yóuzhèng Biānmǎ: 121759). Liánxì Diànhuà: 49940002. Diànzǐ Yóuxiāng: lkuyb@qmnhjvxp.parks.cn

Wei Ji Park, 732 Hao Qiao Road, Sanshui District, Foshan, Guangdong. Postal Code: 121759. Phone Number: 49940002. E-mail: lkuyb@qmnhjvxp.parks.cn

CHAPTER 6: SENTENCES (101-120)

1301。火车站

广东省梅州市平远县强陆路 112 号梅州站（ 邮政编码：750049）。联系电话：22797664。电子邮箱：ohkmn@zlpqgerx.chr.cn

Guǎngdōng Shěng Méizhōu Shì Píng Yuǎn Xiàn Qiǎng Liù Lù 112 Hào Méizōu Zhàn (Yóuzhèng Biānmǎ：750049). Liánxì Diànhuà：22797664. Diànzǐ Yóuxiāng：ohkmn@zlpqgerx.chr.cn

Meizhou Railway Station, 112 Qiang Liu Road, Pingyuan County, Meizhou, Guangdong. Postal Code: 750049. Phone Number：22797664. E-mail：ohkmn@zlpqgerx.chr.cn

1302。公共汽车站

广东省茂名市信宜市咚中路 198 号熔恩站（ 邮政编码：660615）。联系电话：85928050。电子邮箱：yumxn@egxbczym.transport.cn

Guǎngdōng Shěng Màomíng Shì Xìn Yí Shì Dōng Zhòng Lù 198 Hào Róng Ēn Zhàn (Yóuzhèng Biānmǎ：660615). Liánxì Diànhuà：85928050. Diànzǐ Yóuxiāng：yumxn@egxbczym.transport.cn

Rong En Bus Station, 198 Dong Zhong Road, Xinyi City, Maoming, Guangdong. Postal Code: 660615. Phone Number：85928050. E-mail：yumxn@egxbczym.transport.cn

1303。公共汽车站

广东省河源市紫金县化石路 612 号刚浩站（ 邮政编码：817363）。联系电话：61937211。电子邮箱：wxdsl@bcnzteoj.transport.cn

Guǎngdōng Shěng Héyuán Shì Zǐjīn Xiàn Huà Dàn Lù 612 Hào Gāng Hào Zhàn (Yóuzhèng Biānmǎ：817363). Liánxì Diànhuà：61937211. Diànzǐ Yóuxiāng：wxdsl@bcnzteoj.transport.cn

Gang Hao Bus Station, 612 Hua Dan Road, Zijin County, Heyuan, Guangdong. Postal Code: 817363. Phone Number：61937211. E-mail：wxdsl@bcnzteoj.transport.cn

1304。机场

广东省汕头市龙湖区辉坚路 594 号汕头源茂国际机场（ 邮政编码：867135）。联系电话：64060472。电子邮箱：gtikl@rlnotziy.airports.cn

Guǎngdōng Shěng Shàntóu Shì Lónghúqū Huī Jiān Lù 594 Hào àntóu Yuán Mào Guó Jì Jī Chǎng (Yóuzhèng Biānmǎ：867135). Liánxì Diànhuà：64060472. Diànzǐ Yóuxiāng：gtikl@rlnotziy.airports.cn

Shantou Yuan Mao International Airport, 594 Hui Jian Road, Longhu District, Shantou, Guangdong. Postal Code: 867135. Phone Number：64060472. E-mail：gtikl@rlnotziy.airports.cn

1305。湖泊

广东省潮州市湘桥区坚豪路 247 号大懂湖（ 邮政编码：441798）。联系电话：48632962。电子邮箱：ajctu@jogpklus.lakes.cn

Guǎngdōng Shěng Cháozhōu Shì Xiāng Qiáo Qū Jiān Háo Lù 247 Hào Dài Dǒng Hú (Yóuzhèng Biānmǎ：441798). Liánxì Diànhuà：48632962. Diànzǐ Yóuxiāng：ajctu@jogpklus.lakes.cn

Dai Dong Lake, 247 Jian Hao Road, Xiangqiao District, Chaozhou, Guangdong. Postal Code: 441798. Phone Number：48632962. E-mail：ajctu@jogpklus.lakes.cn

1306。公园

广东省湛江市遂溪县甫钊路 351 号不先公园（ 邮政编码：625543）。联系电话：90742408。电子邮箱：mikgd@gltrxjmo.parks.cn

Guǎngdōng Shěng Zhànjiāng Shì Suì Xī Xiàn Fǔ Zhāo Lù 351 Hào Bù Xiān Gōng Yuán（Yóuzhèng Biānmǎ：625543). Liánxì Diànhuà：90742408. Diànzǐ Yóuxiāng：mikgd@gltrxjmo.parks.cn

Bu Xian Park, 351 Fu Zhao Road, Suixi County, Zhanjiang, Guangdong. Postal Code: 625543. Phone Number：90742408. E-mail：mikgd@gltrxjmo.parks.cn

1307。家庭

广东省揭阳市普宁市冕水路 353 号轵金公寓 6 层 655 室（邮政编码：938877）。联系电话：94174427。电子邮箱：mpeoq@ebaiydnf.cn

Guǎngdōng Shěng Jiēyáng Shì Pǔníng Shì Miǎn Shuǐ Lù 353 Hào Shì Jīn Gōng Yù 6 Céng 655 Shì (Yóuzhèng Biānmǎ：938877). Liánxì Diànhuà：94174427. Diànzǐ Yóuxiāng：mpeoq@ebaiydnf.cn

Room# 655, Floor# 6, Shi Jin Apartment, 353 Mian Shui Road, Puning City, Jieyang, Guangdong. Postal Code: 938877. Phone Number：94174427. E-mail：mpeoq@ebaiydnf.cn

1308。火车站

广东省广州市白云区坤盛路 665 号广州站（邮政编码：534663）。联系电话：26835458。电子邮箱：wntbk@fgoqmjae.chr.cn

Guǎngdōng Shěng Guǎngzhōu Shì Báiyún Qū Kūn Shèng Lù 665 Hào Guǎngzōu Zhàn（Yóuzhèng Biānmǎ：534663). Liánxì Diànhuà：26835458. Diànzǐ Yóuxiāng：wntbk@fgoqmjae.chr.cn

Guangzhou Railway Station, 665 Kun Sheng Road, Baiyun District, Guangzhou, Guangdong. Postal Code: 534663. Phone Number：26835458. E-mail：wntbk@fgoqmjae.chr.cn

1309。酒店

广东省广州市番禺区化原路 375 号秀坡酒店（邮政编码：138139）。联系电话：20635835。电子邮箱：wzroa@qlksuwtc.biz.cn

Guǎngdōng Shěng Guǎngzhōu Shì Pānyú Qū Huà Yuán Lù 375 Hào Xiù Pō Jiǔ Diàn (Yóuzhèng Biānmǎ：138139). Liánxì Diànhuà：20635835. Diànzǐ Yóuxiāng：wzroa@qlksuwtc.biz.cn

Xiu Po Hotel, 375 Hua Yuan Road, Panyu District, Guangzhou, Guangdong. Postal Code: 138139. Phone Number：20635835. E-mail：wzroa@qlksuwtc.biz.cn

1310。湖泊

广东省梅州市蕉岭县红铁路 224 号员阳湖（邮政编码：386334）。联系电话：12529099。电子邮箱：idpfz@mjybpaeu.lakes.cn

Guǎngdōng Shěng Méizhōu Shì Jiāo Lǐng Xiàn Hóng Fū Lù 224 Hào Yún Yáng Hú (Yóuzhèng Biānmǎ：386334). Liánxì Diànhuà：12529099. Diànzǐ Yóuxiāng：idpfz@mjybpaeu.lakes.cn

Yun Yang Lake, 224 Hong Fu Road, Jiaoling County, Meizhou, Guangdong. Postal Code: 386334. Phone Number：12529099. E-mail：idpfz@mjybpaeu.lakes.cn

1311。家庭

广东省清远市佛冈县郁可路 731 号葆铁公寓 12 层 430 室（邮政编码：387177）。联系电话：91856453。电子邮箱：wdgnt@rlxbgkci.cn

Guǎngdōng Shěng Qīngyuǎn Shì Fú Gāng Xiàn Yù Kě Lù 731 Hào Bǎo Fū Gōng Yù 12 Céng 430 Shì (Yóuzhèng Biānmǎ：387177). Liánxì Diànhuà：91856453. Diànzǐ Yóuxiāng：wdgnt@rlxbgkci.cn

Room# 430, Floor# 12, Bao Fu Apartment, 731 Yu Ke Road, Fogang County, Qingyuan, Guangdong. Postal Code: 387177. Phone Number：91856453. E-mail：wdgnt@rlxbgkci.cn

1312。家庭

广东省茂名市高州市盛黎路 242 号游郁公寓 5 层 252 室（邮政编码：146552）。联系电话：80493091。电子邮箱：hiwlt@amhkwqeo.cn

Guǎngdōng Shěng Màomíng Shì Gāozhōu Shì Chéng Lí Lù 242 Hào Yóu Yù Gōng Yù 5 Céng 252 Shì (Yóuzhèng Biānmǎ: 146552). Liánxì Diànhuà: 80493091. Diànzǐ Yóuxiāng: hiwlt@amhkwqeo.cn

Room# 252, Floor# 5, You Yu Apartment, 242 Cheng Li Road, Gaozhou, Maoming, Guangdong. Postal Code: 146552. Phone Number: 80493091. E-mail: hiwlt@amhkwqeo.cn

1313。广场

广东省江门市鹤山市胜人路 564 号咚大广场（邮政编码：705379）。联系电话：23735826。电子邮箱：xmbrn@cmdirkbp.squares.cn

Guǎngdōng Shěng Jiāngmén Shì Hèshān Shì Shēng Rén Lù 564 Hào Dōng Dài Guǎng Chǎng (Yóuzhèng Biānmǎ: 705379). Liánxì Diànhuà: 23735826. Diànzǐ Yóuxiāng: xmbrn@cmdirkbp.squares.cn

Dong Dai Square, 564 Sheng Ren Road, Heshan City, Jiangmen, Guangdong. Postal Code: 705379. Phone Number: 23735826. E-mail: xmbrn@cmdirkbp.squares.cn

1314。酒店

广东省中山市稼兆路 797 号帆福酒店（邮政编码：256366）。联系电话：30915693。电子邮箱：ldqui@bqlyrhmj.biz.cn

Guǎngdōng Shěng Zhōngshān Shì Jià Zhào Lù 797 Hào Fān Fú Jiǔ Diàn (Yóuzhèng Biānmǎ: 256366). Liánxì Diànhuà: 30915693. Diànzǐ Yóuxiāng: ldqui@bqlyrhmj.biz.cn

Fan Fu Hotel, 797 Jia Zhao Road, Zhongshan, Guangdong. Postal Code: 256366. Phone Number: 30915693. E-mail: ldqui@bqlyrhmj.biz.cn

1315。机场

广东省河源市源城区强珂路 714 号河源楚涛国际机场（邮政编码：119142）。联系电话：45807274。电子邮箱：ocqkd@kpvjaumt.airports.cn

Guǎngdōng Shěng Héyuán Shì Yuán Chéngqū Qiǎng Kē Lù 714 Hào Héyuán Chǔ Tāo Guó Jì Jī Chǎng （Yóuzhèng Biānmǎ：119142）. Liánxì Diànhuà：45807274. Diànzǐ Yóuxiāng：ocqkd@kpvjaumt.airports.cn

Heyuan Chu Tao International Airport, 714 Qiang Ke Road, Yuancheng District, Heyuan, Guangdong. Postal Code: 119142. Phone Number：45807274. E-mail：ocqkd@kpvjaumt.airports.cn

1316。湖泊

广东省茂名市电白区乙兵路 386 号帆食湖（邮政编码：249235）。联系电话：71120162。电子邮箱：uhctv@fonxydzv.lakes.cn

Guǎngdōng Shěng Màomíng Shì Diàn Bái Qū Yǐ Bīng Lù 386 Hào Fān Yì Hú （Yóuzhèng Biānmǎ：249235). Liánxì Diànhuà：71120162. Diànzǐ Yóuxiāng：uhctv@fonxydzv.lakes.cn

Fan Yi Lake, 386 Yi Bing Road, Dianbai District, Maoming, Guangdong. Postal Code: 249235. Phone Number：71120162. E-mail：uhctv@fonxydzv.lakes.cn

1317。湖泊

广东省阳江市江城区谢恩路 737 号成近湖（邮政编码：117928）。联系电话：57906365。电子邮箱：ofesz@htbaiczq.lakes.cn

Guǎngdōng Shěng Yángjiāng Shì Jiāng Chéngqū Xiè Ēn Lù 737 Hào Chéng Jìn Hú （Yóuzhèng Biānmǎ：117928). Liánxì Diànhuà：57906365. Diànzǐ Yóuxiāng：ofesz@htbaiczq.lakes.cn

Cheng Jin Lake, 737 Xie En Road, Jiangcheng District, Yangjiang, Guangdong. Postal Code: 117928. Phone Number：57906365. E-mail：ofesz@htbaiczq.lakes.cn

1318。寺庙

广东省韶关市乐昌市己民路 184 号铭立寺（邮政编码：329158）。联系电话：38137318。电子邮箱：gcydv@tbczmqed.god.cn

Guǎngdōng Shěng Sháoguān Shì Lè Chāng Shì Jǐ Mín Lù 184 Hào Míng Lì Sì (Yóuzhèng Biānmǎ：329158). Liánxì Diànhuà：38137318. Diànzǐ Yóuxiāng：gcydv@tbczmqed.god.cn

Ming Li Temple, 184 Ji Min Road, Lechang City, Shaoguan, Guangdong. Postal Code: 329158. Phone Number：38137318. E-mail：gcydv@tbczmqed.god.cn

1319。大学

广东省揭阳市普宁市尚跃大学茂人路 550 号（邮政编码：636221）。联系电话：81897464。电子邮箱：evdta@jfuqbxno.edu.cn

Guǎngdōng Shěng Jiēyáng Shì Pǔníng Shì Shàng Yuè DàxuéMào Rén Lù 550 Hào (Yóuzhèng Biānmǎ：636221). Liánxì Diànhuà：81897464. Diànzǐ Yóuxiāng：evdta@jfuqbxno.edu.cn

Shang Yue University, 550 Mao Ren Road, Puning City, Jieyang, Guangdong. Postal Code: 636221. Phone Number：81897464. E-mail：evdta@jfuqbxno.edu.cn

1320。广场

广东省梅州市大埔县翼葛路 320 号风庆广场（邮政编码：831486）。联系电话：72167469。电子邮箱：feuta@mztyolif.squares.cn

Guǎngdōng Shěng Méizhōu Shì Dà Bù Xiàn Yì Gé Lù 320 Hào Fēng Qìng Guǎng Chǎng (Yóuzhèng Biānmǎ：831486). Liánxì Diànhuà：72167469. Diànzǐ Yóuxiāng：feuta@mztyolif.squares.cn

Feng Qing Square, 320 Yi Ge Road, Dapu County, Meizhou, Guangdong. Postal Code: 831486. Phone Number：72167469. E-mail：feuta@mztyolif.squares.cn

CHAPTER 7: SENTENCES (121-140)

1321。机场

广东省东莞市隆锡路 808 号东莞亚不国际机场（邮政编码：426321）。联系电话：28239968。电子邮箱：hxmiq@uaeqnbtp.airports.cn

Guǎngdōng Shěng Dōngguǎn Shì Lóng Xī Lù 808 Hào Dōngguǎn Yà Bù Guó Jì Jī Chǎng （Yóuzhèng Biānmǎ：426321). Liánxì Diànhuà：28239968. Diànzǐ Yóuxiāng：hxmiq@uaeqnbtp.airports.cn

Dongguan Ya Bu International Airport, 808 Long Xi Road, Dongguan, Guangdong. Postal Code: 426321. Phone Number：28239968. E-mail：hxmiq@uaeqnbtp.airports.cn

1322。公园

广东省东莞市桥宝路 681 号顺腾公园（邮政编码：325539）。联系电话：43671339。电子邮箱：ljasg@yphguxst.parks.cn

Guǎngdōng Shěng Dōngguǎn Shì Qiáo Bǎo Lù 681 Hào Shùn Téng Gōng Yuán (Yóuzhèng Biānmǎ：325539). Liánxì Diànhuà：43671339. Diànzǐ Yóuxiāng：ljasg@yphguxst.parks.cn

Shun Teng Park, 681 Qiao Bao Road, Dongguan, Guangdong. Postal Code: 325539. Phone Number：43671339. E-mail：ljasg@yphguxst.parks.cn

1323。医院

广东省广州市荔湾区沛沛路 714 号黎斌医院（邮政编码：160386）。联系电话：76009902。电子邮箱：vkfpb@bxlscyjf.health.cn

Guǎngdōng Shěng Guǎngzhōu Shì Lìwān Qū Pèi Pèi Lù 714 Hào Lí Bīn Yī Yuàn (Yóuzhèng Biānmǎ：160386). Liánxì Diànhuà：76009902. Diànzǐ Yóuxiāng：vkfpb@bxlscyjf.health.cn

Li Bin Hospital, 714 Pei Pei Road, Liwan District, Guangzhou, Guangdong. Postal Code: 160386. Phone Number：76009902. E-mail：vkfpb@bxlscyjf.health.cn

1324。公共汽车站

广东省茂名市化州市智豪路 116 号自食站（ 邮政编码：387125）。联系电话：18806641。电子邮箱：wckpz@qfdepohr.transport.cn

Guǎngdōng Shěng Màomíng Shì Huà Zhōu Shì Zhì Háo Lù 116 Hào Zì Shí Zhàn (Yóuzhèng Biānmǎ：387125). Liánxì Diànhuà：18806641. Diànzǐ Yóuxiāng：wckpz@qfdepohr.transport.cn

Zi Shi Bus Station, 116 Zhi Hao Road, Huazhou, Maoming, Guangdong. Postal Code: 387125. Phone Number：18806641. E-mail：wckpz@qfdepohr.transport.cn

1325。寺庙

广东省广州市黄埔区振彬路 241 号院轶寺（ 邮政编码：513235）。联系电话：25331381。电子邮箱：qmdbh@putgdbxe.god.cn

Guǎngdōng Shěng Guǎngzhōu Shì Huángbù Qū Zhèn Bīn Lù 241 Hào Yuàn Yì Sì (Yóuzhèng Biānmǎ：513235). Liánxì Diànhuà：25331381. Diànzǐ Yóuxiāng：qmdbh@putgdbxe.god.cn

Yuan Yi Temple, 241 Zhen Bin Road, Huangpu District, Guangzhou, Guangdong. Postal Code: 513235. Phone Number：25331381. E-mail：qmdbh@putgdbxe.god.cn

1326。家庭

广东省梅州市梅江区祥世路 928 号轶楚公寓 32 层 867 室（ 邮政编码：828307）。联系电话：87965432。电子邮箱：hbisn@tnefbuxk.cn

Guǎngdōng Shěng Méizhōu Shì Méi Jiāng Qū Xiáng Shì Lù 928 Hào Yì Chǔ Gōng Yù 32 Céng 867 Shì (Yóuzhèng Biānmǎ：828307). Liánxì Diànhuà：87965432. Diànzǐ Yóuxiāng：hbisn@tnefbuxk.cn

Room# 867, Floor# 32, Yi Chu Apartment, 928 Xiang Shi Road, Meijiang District, Meizhou, Guangdong. Postal Code: 828307. Phone Number：87965432. E-mail：hbisn@tnefbuxk.cn

1327。公司

广东省潮州市潮安区民阳路 993 号威炯有限公司（邮政编码：422672）。联系电话：33002233。电子邮箱：acokz@wospdjxa.biz.cn

Guǎngdōng Shěng Cháozhōu Shì Cháo Ān Qū Mín Yáng Lù 993 Hào Wēi Jiǒng Yǒuxiàn Gōngsī (Yóuzhèng Biānmǎ：422672). Liánxì Diànhuà：33002233. Diànzǐ Yóuxiāng：acokz@wospdjxa.biz.cn

Wei Jiong Corporation, 993 Min Yang Road, Chaoan District, Chaozhou, Guangdong. Postal Code: 422672. Phone Number：33002233. E-mail：acokz@wospdjxa.biz.cn

1328。大学

广东省东莞市锤盛大学原腾路 417 号（邮政编码：766591）。联系电话：28392968。电子邮箱：cxlyj@bouimlhc.edu.cn

Guǎngdōng Shěng Dōngguǎn Shì Chuí Chéng DàxuéYuán Téng Lù 417 Hào (Yóuzhèng Biānmǎ：766591). Liánxì Diànhuà：28392968. Diànzǐ Yóuxiāng：cxlyj@bouimlhc.edu.cn

Chui Cheng University, 417 Yuan Teng Road, Dongguan, Guangdong. Postal Code: 766591. Phone Number：28392968. E-mail：cxlyj@bouimlhc.edu.cn

1329。火车站

广东省肇庆市鼎湖区启锡路 158 号肇庆站（邮政编码：665006）。联系电话：25431534。电子邮箱：elrvm@cuohvmta.chr.cn

Guǎngdōng Shěng Zhàoqìng Shì Dǐng Hú Qū Qǐ Xī Lù 158 Hào Zàoqng Zhàn (Yóuzhèng Biānmǎ： 665006). Liánxì Diànhuà： 25431534. Diànzǐ Yóuxiāng： elrvm@cuohvmta.chr.cn

Zhaoqing Railway Station, 158 Qi Xi Road, Dinghu District, Zhaoqing, Guangdong. Postal Code: 665006. Phone Number： 25431534. E-mail： elrvm@cuohvmta.chr.cn

1330。大学

广东省中山市郁珏大学郁冠路 839 号（邮政编码：904180）。联系电话：96144313。电子邮箱：oxqbj@cbqfoeuk.edu.cn

Guǎngdōng Shěng Zhōngshān Shì Yù Jué DàxuéYù Guàn Lù 839 Hào (Yóuzhèng Biānmǎ： 904180). Liánxì Diànhuà： 96144313. Diànzǐ Yóuxiāng： oxqbj@cbqfoeuk.edu.cn

Yu Jue University, 839 Yu Guan Road, Zhongshan, Guangdong. Postal Code: 904180. Phone Number： 96144313. E-mail： oxqbj@cbqfoeuk.edu.cn

1331。博物院

广东省清远市佛冈县奎葆路 170 号清远博物馆（邮政编码：603032）。联系电话：84626916。电子邮箱：eslim@juqpecgo.museums.cn

Guǎngdōng Shěng Qīngyuǎn Shì Fú Gāng Xiàn Kuí Bǎo Lù 170 Hào Qīngyuǎn Bó Wù Guǎn (Yóuzhèng Biānmǎ： 603032). Liánxì Diànhuà： 84626916. Diànzǐ Yóuxiāng： eslim@juqpecgo.museums.cn

Qingyuan Museum, 170 Kui Bao Road, Fogang County, Qingyuan, Guangdong. Postal Code: 603032. Phone Number： 84626916. E-mail： eslim@juqpecgo.museums.cn

1332。公共汽车站

广东省阳江市阳春市圣臻路 868 号己智站（ 邮政编码：804457）。联系电话：29345062。电子邮箱：wysxe@pfrentjq.transport.cn

Guǎngdōng Shěng Yángjiāng Shì Yángchūn Shì Shèng Zhēn Lù 868 Hào Jǐ Zhì Zhàn (Yóuzhèng Biānmǎ：804457). Liánxì Diànhuà：29345062. Diànzǐ Yóuxiāng：wysxe@pfrentjq.transport.cn

Ji Zhi Bus Station, 868 Sheng Zhen Road, Yangchun City, Yangjiang, Guangdong. Postal Code: 804457. Phone Number：29345062. E-mail：wysxe@pfrentjq.transport.cn

1333。寺庙

广东省汕尾市陆丰市石钦路 481 号岐友寺（ 邮政编码：921054）。联系电话：42448070。电子邮箱：hsqtb@gzwinacj.god.cn

Guǎngdōng Shěng Shànwěi Shì Lùfēng Shì Shí Qīn Lù 481 Hào Qí Yǒu Sì (Yóuzhèng Biānmǎ：921054). Liánxì Diànhuà：42448070. Diànzǐ Yóuxiāng：hsqtb@gzwinacj.god.cn

Qi You Temple, 481 Shi Qin Road, Lufeng, Shanwei, Guangdong. Postal Code: 921054. Phone Number：42448070. E-mail：hsqtb@gzwinacj.god.cn

1334。公司

广东省汕头市南澳县骥继路 683 号兵舟有限公司（ 邮政编码：371125）。联系电话：23883465。电子邮箱：szbrx@tsgjyedm.biz.cn

Guǎngdōng Shěng Shàntóu Shì Nán'ào Xiàn Jì Jì Lù 683 Hào Bīng Zhōu Yǒuxiàn Gōngsī (Yóuzhèng Biānmǎ：371125). Liánxì Diànhuà：23883465. Diànzǐ Yóuxiāng：szbrx@tsgjyedm.biz.cn

Bing Zhou Corporation, 683 Ji Ji Road, Nan'ao County, Shantou, Guangdong. Postal Code: 371125. Phone Number：23883465. E-mail：szbrx@tsgjyedm.biz.cn

1335。公共汽车站

广东省珠海市香洲区继宽路 502 号阳鸣站（ 邮政编码：772220）。联系电话：35384517。电子邮箱：vxwjz@gwymxzhc.transport.cn

Guǎngdōng Shěng Zhūhǎi Shì Xiāngzhōu Qū Jì Kuān Lù 502 Hào Yáng Míng Zhàn (Yóuzhèng Biānmǎ：772220). Liánxì Diànhuà：35384517. Diànzǐ Yóuxiāng：vxwjz@gwymxzhc.transport.cn

Yang Ming Bus Station, 502 Ji Kuan Road, Xiangzhou District, Zhuhai, Guangdong. Postal Code: 772220. Phone Number：35384517. E-mail：vxwjz@gwymxzhc.transport.cn

1336。公园

广东省惠州市博罗县可智路 186 号甫人公园（ 邮政编码：565666）。联系电话：56809518。电子邮箱：bmthc@ibfzjomp.parks.cn

Guǎngdōng Shěng Huìzhōu Shì Bó Luō Xiàn Kě Zhì Lù 186 Hào Fǔ Rén Gōng Yuán (Yóuzhèng Biānmǎ：565666). Liánxì Diànhuà：56809518. Diànzǐ Yóuxiāng：bmthc@ibfzjomp.parks.cn

Fu Ren Park, 186 Ke Zhi Road, Boluo County, Huizhou, Guangdong. Postal Code: 565666. Phone Number：56809518. E-mail：bmthc@ibfzjomp.parks.cn

1337。家庭

广东省云浮市云城区钢土路 602 号胜甫公寓 18 层 435 室（ 邮政编码：497302）。联系电话：45030180。电子邮箱：juazf@idjhbvyn.cn

Guǎngdōng Shěng Yúnfú Shì Yún Chéngqū Gāng Tǔ Lù 602 Hào Shèng Fǔ Gōng Yù 18 Céng 435 Shì (Yóuzhèng Biānmǎ：497302). Liánxì Diànhuà：45030180. Diànzǐ Yóuxiāng：juazf@idjhbvyn.cn

Room# 435, Floor# 18, Sheng Fu Apartment, 602 Gang Tu Road, Yuncheng District, Yunfu, Guangdong. Postal Code: 497302. Phone Number：45030180. E-mail：juazf@idjhbvyn.cn

1338。博物院

广东省阳江市阳西县仓屹路 973 号阳江博物馆（邮政编码：625487）。联系电话：68088772。电子邮箱：bqsxp@pgauwbif.museums.cn

Guǎngdōng Shěng Yángjiāng Shì Yáng Xī Xiàn Cāng Yì Lù 973 Hào Yángjiāng Bó Wù Guǎn (Yóuzhèng Biānmǎ：625487). Liánxì Diànhuà：68088772. Diànzǐ Yóuxiāng：bqsxp@pgauwbif.museums.cn

Yangjiang Museum, 973 Cang Yi Road, Yangxi County, Yangjiang, Guangdong. Postal Code: 625487. Phone Number：68088772. E-mail：bqsxp@pgauwbif.museums.cn

1339。酒店

广东省梅州市梅江区守黎路 507 号甫金酒店（邮政编码：190108）。联系电话：19108875。电子邮箱：vhjfu@yseaqiuv.biz.cn

Guǎngdōng Shěng Méizhōu Shì Méi Jiāng Qū Shǒu Lí Lù 507 Hào Fǔ Jīn Jiǔ Diàn (Yóuzhèng Biānmǎ：190108). Liánxì Diànhuà：19108875. Diànzǐ Yóuxiāng：vhjfu@yseaqiuv.biz.cn

Fu Jin Hotel, 507 Shou Li Road, Meijiang District, Meizhou, Guangdong. Postal Code: 190108. Phone Number：19108875. E-mail：vhjfu@yseaqiuv.biz.cn

1340。广场

广东省佛山市三水区轼焯路 962 号沛祥广场（邮政编码：348339）。联系电话：47971679。电子邮箱：paorm@widysjph.squares.cn

Guǎngdōng Shěng Fúshān Shì Sān Shuǐ Qū Shì Zhuō Lù 962 Hào Pèi Xiáng Guǎng Chǎng (Yóuzhèng Biānmǎ：348339). Liánxì Diànhuà：47971679. Diànzǐ Yóuxiāng：paorm@widysjph.squares.cn

Pei Xiang Square, 962 Shi Zhuo Road, Sanshui District, Foshan, Guangdong. Postal Code: 348339. Phone Number：47971679. E-mail：paorm@widysjph.squares.cn

CHAPTER 8: SENTENCES (141-160)

1341。寺庙

广东省佛山市南海区石珏路 649 号克乙寺（邮政编码：961396）。联系电话：28368550。电子邮箱：mjlfg@sknlzbut.god.cn

Guǎngdōng Shěng Fúshān Shì Nánhǎi Qū Shí Jué Lù 649 Hào Kè Yǐ Sì (Yóuzhèng Biānmǎ：961396). Liánxì Diànhuà：28368550. Diànzǐ Yóuxiāng：mjlfg@sknlzbut.god.cn

Ke Yi Temple, 649 Shi Jue Road, Nanhai District, Foshan, Guangdong. Postal Code: 961396. Phone Number：28368550. E-mail：mjlfg@sknlzbut.god.cn

1342。公共汽车站

广东省韶关市翁源县福洵路 622 号铁俊站（邮政编码：646255）。联系电话：72907632。电子邮箱：reucq@bxemipag.transport.cn

Guǎngdōng Shěng Sháoguān Shì Wēng Yuán Xiàn Fú Xún Lù 622 Hào Fū Jùn Zhàn (Yóuzhèng Biānmǎ：646255). Liánxì Diànhuà：72907632. Diànzǐ Yóuxiāng：reucq@bxemipag.transport.cn

Fu Jun Bus Station, 622 Fu Xun Road, Wengyuan County, Shaoguan, Guangdong. Postal Code: 646255. Phone Number：72907632. E-mail：reucq@bxemipag.transport.cn

1343。家庭

广东省清远市佛冈县豪中路 865 号祥冕公寓 12 层 689 室（邮政编码：167943）。联系电话：95122696。电子邮箱：bftvs@kbicymeq.cn

Guǎngdōng Shěng Qīngyuǎn Shì Fú Gāng Xiàn Háo Zhōng Lù 865 Hào Xiáng Miǎn Gōng Yù 12 Céng 689 Shì (Yóuzhèng Biānmǎ：167943). Liánxì Diànhuà：95122696. Diànzǐ Yóuxiāng：bftvs@kbicymeq.cn

Room# 689, Floor# 12, Xiang Mian Apartment, 865 Hao Zhong Road, Fogang County, Qingyuan, Guangdong. Postal Code: 167943. Phone Number：95122696. E-mail：bftvs@kbicymeq.cn

1344。公司

广东省珠海市香洲区盛全路 800 号冠金有限公司（邮政编码：705433）。联系电话：47362018。电子邮箱：mdgke@hpcwydil.biz.cn

Guǎngdōng Shěng Zhūhǎi Shì Xiāngzhōu Qū Chéng Quán Lù 800 Hào Guān Jīn Yǒuxiàn Gōngsī (Yóuzhèng Biānmǎ：705433). Liánxì Diànhuà：47362018. Diànzǐ Yóuxiāng：mdgke@hpcwydil.biz.cn

Guan Jin Corporation, 800 Cheng Quan Road, Xiangzhou District, Zhuhai, Guangdong. Postal Code: 705433. Phone Number：47362018. E-mail：mdgke@hpcwydil.biz.cn

1345。广场

广东省深圳市福田区土盛路 348 号桥铭广场（邮政编码：297037）。联系电话：72626101。电子邮箱：hwize@awluyzcr.squares.cn

Guǎngdōng Shěng Shēnzhèn Shì Fútián Qū Tǔ Shèng Lù 348 Hào Qiáo Míng Guǎng Chǎng (Yóuzhèng Biānmǎ：297037). Liánxì Diànhuà：72626101. Diànzǐ Yóuxiāng：hwize@awluyzcr.squares.cn

Qiao Ming Square, 348 Tu Sheng Road, Futian District, Shenzhen, Guangdong. Postal Code: 297037. Phone Number：72626101. E-mail：hwize@awluyzcr.squares.cn

1346。机场

广东省清远市阳山县居大路 658 号清远顺化国际机场（邮政编码：551142）。联系电话：90948461。电子邮箱：zgnif@sctweakn.airports.cn

Guǎngdōng Shěng Qīngyuǎn Shì Yáng Shānxiàn Jū Dà Lù 658 Hào Qīngyuǎn Shùn Huà Guó Jì Jī Chǎng (Yóuzhèng Biānmǎ: 551142). Liánxì Diànhuà: 90948461. Diànzǐ Yóuxiāng: zgnif@sctweakn.airports.cn

Qingyuan Shun Hua International Airport, 658 Ju Da Road, Yangshan County, Qingyuan, Guangdong. Postal Code: 551142. Phone Number: 90948461. E-mail: zgnif@sctweakn.airports.cn

1347。家庭

广东省云浮市郁南县星沛路 977 号冠独公寓 22 层 846 室（邮政编码：791519）。联系电话：25368064。电子邮箱：vhlso@zrpqakbf.cn

Guǎngdōng Shěng Yúnfú Shì Yù Nán Xiàn Xīng Pèi Lù 977 Hào Guàn Dú Gōng Yù 22 Céng 846 Shì (Yóuzhèng Biānmǎ: 791519). Liánxì Diànhuà: 25368064. Diànzǐ Yóuxiāng: vhlso@zrpqakbf.cn

Room# 846, Floor# 22, Guan Du Apartment, 977 Xing Pei Road, Yunan County, Yunfu, Guangdong. Postal Code: 791519. Phone Number: 25368064. E-mail: vhlso@zrpqakbf.cn

1348。寺庙

广东省汕尾市海丰县钊陶路 205 号启晗寺（邮政编码：414888）。联系电话：61468226。电子邮箱：bisut@tipnrlfx.god.cn

Guǎngdōng Shěng Shànwěi Shì Hǎi Fēngxiàn Zhāo Táo Lù 205 Hào Qǐ Hán Sì (Yóuzhèng Biānmǎ: 414888). Liánxì Diànhuà: 61468226. Diànzǐ Yóuxiāng: bisut@tipnrlfx.god.cn

Qi Han Temple, 205 Zhao Tao Road, Haifeng County, Shanwei, Guangdong. Postal Code: 414888. Phone Number: 61468226. E-mail: bisut@tipnrlfx.god.cn

1349。大学

广东省东莞市独中大学坤陶路 522 号（邮政编码：987562）。联系电话：58237778。电子邮箱：sfvzj@musygcht.edu.cn

Guăngdōng Shěng Dōngguǎn Shì Dú Zhōng DàxuéKūn Táo Lù 522 Hào（Yóuzhèng Biānmǎ：987562). Liánxì Diànhuà：58237778. Diànzǐ Yóuxiāng：sfvzj@musygcht.edu.cn

Du Zhong University, 522 Kun Tao Road, Dongguan, Guangdong. Postal Code: 987562. Phone Number：58237778. E-mail：sfvzj@musygcht.edu.cn

1350。医院

广东省梅州市梅县区歧楚路 166 号茂成医院（邮政编码：362478）。联系电话：67680697。电子邮箱：urjfb@tsdepwfn.health.cn

Guăngdōng Shěng Méizhōu Shì Méixiàn Qū Qí Chǔ Lù 166 Hào Mào Chéng Yī Yuàn（Yóuzhèng Biānmǎ：362478). Liánxì Diànhuà：67680697. Diànzǐ Yóuxiāng：urjfb@tsdepwfn.health.cn

Mao Cheng Hospital, 166 Qi Chu Road, Meixian District, Meizhou, Guangdong. Postal Code: 362478. Phone Number：67680697. E-mail：urjfb@tsdepwfn.health.cn

1351。公司

广东省汕头市龙湖区立鸣路 140 号渊陆有限公司（邮政编码：246003）。联系电话：24431428。电子邮箱：tqufl@lweopmja.biz.cn

Guăngdōng Shěng Shàntóu Shì Lónghúqū Lì Míng Lù 140 Hào Yuān Liù Yǒuxiàn Gōngsī（Yóuzhèng Biānmǎ：246003). Liánxì Diànhuà：24431428. Diànzǐ Yóuxiāng：tqufl@lweopmja.biz.cn

Yuan Liu Corporation, 140 Li Ming Road, Longhu District, Shantou, Guangdong. Postal Code: 246003. Phone Number：24431428. E-mail：tqufl@lweopmja.biz.cn

1352。大学

广东省韶关市武江区斌化大学盛胜路 143 号（邮政编码：545088）。联系电话：11594467。电子邮箱：kdytl@wpxfoeuy.edu.cn

Guǎngdōng Shěng Sháoguān Shì Wǔjiāng Qū Bīn Huà DàxuéChéng Shēng Lù 143 Hào（Yóuzhèng Biānmǎ：545088). Liánxì Diànhuà：11594467. Diànzǐ Yóuxiāng：kdytl@wpxfoeuy.edu.cn

Bin Hua University, 143 Cheng Sheng Road, Wujiang District, Shaoguan, Guangdong. Postal Code: 545088. Phone Number：11594467. E-mail：kdytl@wpxfoeuy.edu.cn

1353。酒店

广东省深圳市南山区敬禹路 630 号愈大酒店（邮政编码：819065）。联系电话：90952981。电子邮箱：qahux@cklahnis.biz.cn

Guǎngdōng Shěng Shēnzhèn Shì Nánshānqū Jìng Yǔ Lù 630 Hào Yù Dài Jiǔ Diàn（Yóuzhèng Biānmǎ：819065). Liánxì Diànhuà：90952981. Diànzǐ Yóuxiāng：qahux@cklahnis.biz.cn

Yu Dai Hotel, 630 Jing Yu Road, Nanshan District, Shenzhen, Guangdong. Postal Code: 819065. Phone Number：90952981. E-mail：qahux@cklahnis.biz.cn

1354。博物院

广东省汕尾市陆河县冠金路 435 号汕尾博物馆（邮政编码：285421）。联系电话：15823046。电子邮箱：gcwuy@krzgsnhu.museums.cn

Guǎngdōng Shěng Shànwěi Shì Lù Hé Xiàn Guān Jīn Lù 435 Hào ànwěi Bó Wù Guǎn（Yóuzhèng Biānmǎ：285421). Liánxì Diànhuà：15823046. Diànzǐ Yóuxiāng：gcwuy@krzgsnhu.museums.cn

Shanwei Museum, 435 Guan Jin Road, Luhe County, Shanwei, Guangdong. Postal Code: 285421. Phone Number：15823046. E-mail：gcwuy@krzgsnhu.museums.cn

1355。博物院

广东省惠州市惠东县辙光路 310 号惠州博物馆（邮政编码：408883）。联系电话：83058981。电子邮箱：igvlr@zckfimgj.museums.cn

Guǎngdōng Shěng Huìzhōu Shì Huì Dōng Xiàn Zhé Guāng Lù 310 Hào Huzōu Bó Wù Guǎn (Yóuzhèng Biānmǎ：408883). Liánxì Diànhuà：83058981. Diànzǐ Yóuxiāng：igvlr@zckfimgj.museums.cn

Huizhou Museum, 310 Zhe Guang Road, Huidong County, Huizhou, Guangdong. Postal Code: 408883. Phone Number：83058981. E-mail：igvlr@zckfimgj.museums.cn

1356。公共汽车站

广东省河源市源城区征辉路 279 号庆学站（邮政编码：855618）。联系电话：46074820。电子邮箱：ebvmu@exzvjahd.transport.cn

Guǎngdōng Shěng Héyuán Shì Yuán Chéngqū Zhēng Huī Lù 279 Hào Qìng Xué Zhàn (Yóuzhèng Biānmǎ：855618). Liánxì Diànhuà：46074820. Diànzǐ Yóuxiāng：ebvmu@exzvjahd.transport.cn

Qing Xue Bus Station, 279 Zheng Hui Road, Yuancheng District, Heyuan, Guangdong. Postal Code: 855618. Phone Number：46074820. E-mail：ebvmu@exzvjahd.transport.cn

1357。公共汽车站

广东省广州市花都区淘乙路 336 号不来站（邮政编码：427870）。联系电话：72374879。电子邮箱：pcghs@kyhfcvmi.transport.cn

Guǎngdōng Shěng Guǎngzhōu Shì Huā Dū Qū Xún Yǐ Lù 336 Hào Bù Lái Zhàn (Yóuzhèng Biānmǎ: 427870). Liánxì Diànhuà: 72374879. Diànzǐ Yóuxiāng: pcghs@kyhfcvmi.transport.cn

Bu Lai Bus Station, 336 Xun Yi Road, Huadu District, Guangzhou, Guangdong. Postal Code: 427870. Phone Number: 72374879. E-mail: pcghs@kyhfcvmi.transport.cn

1358。酒店

广东省揭阳市揭东区岐红路 573 号钢锤酒店（邮政编码：825984）。联系电话：31253591。电子邮箱：phljt@qivpubdm.biz.cn

Guǎngdōng Shěng Jiēyáng Shì Jiē Dōngqū Qí Hóng Lù 573 Hào Gāng Chuí Jiǔ Diàn (Yóuzhèng Biānmǎ: 825984). Liánxì Diànhuà: 31253591. Diànzǐ Yóuxiāng: phljt@qivpubdm.biz.cn

Gang Chui Hotel, 573 Qi Hong Road, Jiedong District, Jieyang, Guangdong. Postal Code: 825984. Phone Number: 31253591. E-mail: phljt@qivpubdm.biz.cn

1359。火车站

广东省深圳市宝安区锤星路 924 号深圳站（邮政编码：774186）。联系电话：56175722。电子邮箱：eraxq@exwqbzso.chr.cn

Guǎngdōng Shěng Shēnzhèn Shì Bǎo'ān Qū Chuí Xīng Lù 924 Hào ēnzèn Zhàn (Yóuzhèng Biānmǎ: 774186). Liánxì Diànhuà: 56175722. Diànzǐ Yóuxiāng: eraxq@exwqbzso.chr.cn

Shenzhen Railway Station, 924 Chui Xing Road, Bao'an District, Shenzhen, Guangdong. Postal Code: 774186. Phone Number: 56175722. E-mail: eraxq@exwqbzso.chr.cn

1360。公共汽车站

广东省惠州市惠阳区钢乙路 484 号兵智站（ 邮政编码：600643）。联系电话：88958086。电子邮箱：dtvcr@hvfmbntk.transport.cn

Guǎngdōng Shěng Huìzhōu Shì Huìyáng Qū Gāng Yǐ Lù 484 Hào Bīng Zhì Zhàn (Yóuzhèng Biānmǎ：600643). Liánxì Diànhuà：88958086. Diànzǐ Yóuxiāng：dtvcr@hvfmbntk.transport.cn

Bing Zhi Bus Station, 484 Gang Yi Road, Huiyang District, Huizhou, Guangdong. Postal Code: 600643. Phone Number：88958086. E-mail：dtvcr@hvfmbntk.transport.cn

CHAPTER 9: SENTENCES (161-180)

1361。医院

广东省广州市花都区大其路 254 号强沛医院（邮政编码：456584）。联系电话：96809736。电子邮箱：ceayl@jliprsht.health.cn

Guǎngdōng Shěng Guǎngzhōu Shì Huā Dū Qū Dài Qí Lù 254 Hào Qiǎng Pèi Yī Yuàn (Yóuzhèng Biānmǎ：456584). Liánxì Diànhuà：96809736. Diànzǐ Yóuxiāng：ceayl@jliprsht.health.cn

Qiang Pei Hospital, 254 Dai Qi Road, Huadu District, Guangzhou, Guangdong. Postal Code: 456584. Phone Number：96809736. E-mail：ceayl@jliprsht.health.cn

1362。机场

广东省河源市紫金县懂甫路 275 号河源秀顺国际机场（邮政编码：194457）。联系电话：37096640。电子邮箱：kmqej@ekzamgfc.airports.cn

Guǎngdōng Shěng Héyuán Shì Zǐjīn Xiàn Dǒng Fǔ Lù 275 Hào Héyuán Xiù Shùn Guó Jì Jī Chǎng (Yóuzhèng Biānmǎ：194457). Liánxì Diànhuà：37096640. Diànzǐ Yóuxiāng：kmqej@ekzamgfc.airports.cn

Heyuan Xiu Shun International Airport, 275 Dong Fu Road, Zijin County, Heyuan, Guangdong. Postal Code: 194457. Phone Number：37096640. E-mail：kmqej@ekzamgfc.airports.cn

1363。湖泊

广东省江门市蓬江区淹淹路 903 号茂岐湖（邮政编码：448852）。联系电话：22073747。电子邮箱：vcgdw@ysxgrqza.lakes.cn

Guǎngdōng Shěng Jiāngmén Shì Péng Jiāng Qū Yān Yān Lù 903 Hào Mào Qí Hú (Yóuzhèng Biānmǎ：448852). Liánxì Diànhuà：22073747. Diànzǐ Yóuxiāng：vcgdw@ysxgrqza.lakes.cn

Mao Qi Lake, 903 Yan Yan Road, Pengjiang District, Jiangmen, Guangdong. Postal Code: 448852. Phone Number：22073747. E-mail：vcgdw@ysxgrqza.lakes.cn

1364。湖泊

广东省汕尾市海丰县翰院路 841 号继嘉湖（ 邮政编码：491690）。联系电话：38935558。电子邮箱：njbcz@anyrfkmq.lakes.cn

Guǎngdōng Shěng Shànwěi Shì Hǎi Fēngxiàn Hàn Yuàn Lù 841 Hào Jì Jiā Hú (Yóuzhèng Biānmǎ：491690). Liánxì Diànhuà：38935558. Diànzǐ Yóuxiāng：njbcz@anyrfkmq.lakes.cn

Ji Jia Lake, 841 Han Yuan Road, Haifeng County, Shanwei, Guangdong. Postal Code: 491690. Phone Number：38935558. E-mail：njbcz@anyrfkmq.lakes.cn

1365。酒店

广东省惠州市博罗县进化路 863 号鸣兵酒店（ 邮政编码：773469）。联系电话：76512501。电子邮箱：enmia@wjzgiyvm.biz.cn

Guǎngdōng Shěng Huìzhōu Shì Bó Luō Xiàn Jìn Huà Lù 863 Hào Míng Bīng Jiǔ Diàn (Yóuzhèng Biānmǎ：773469). Liánxì Diànhuà：76512501. Diànzǐ Yóuxiāng：enmia@wjzgiyvm.biz.cn

Ming Bing Hotel, 863 Jin Hua Road, Boluo County, Huizhou, Guangdong. Postal Code: 773469. Phone Number：76512501. E-mail：enmia@wjzgiyvm.biz.cn

1366。博物院

广东省佛山市禅城区毅嘉路 741 号佛山博物馆（ 邮政编码：696627）。联系电话：58471958。电子邮箱：rnamu@fthcnodl.museums.cn

Guǎngdōng Shěng Fúshān Shì Chán Chéngqū Yì Jiā Lù 741 Hào Fúsān Bó Wù Guǎn (Yóuzhèng Biānmǎ：696627). Liánxì Diànhuà：58471958. Diànzǐ Yóuxiāng：rnamu@fthcnodl.museums.cn

Foshan Museum, 741 Yi Jia Road, Chancheng District, Foshan, Guangdong. Postal Code: 696627. Phone Number：58471958. E-mail：rnamu@fthcnodl.museums.cn

1367。大学

广东省湛江市霞山区尚胜大学成科路 209 号（邮政编码：537049）。联系电话：90081736。电子邮箱：bympz@ycnzaegj.edu.cn

Guǎngdōng Shěng Zhànjiāng Shì Xiá Shānqū Shàng Shēng DàxuéChéng Kē Lù 209 Hào（Yóuzhèng Biānmǎ：537049). Liánxì Diànhuà：90081736. Diànzǐ Yóuxiāng：bympz@ycnzaegj.edu.cn

Shang Sheng University, 209 Cheng Ke Road, Xiashan District, Zhanjiang, Guangdong. Postal Code: 537049. Phone Number：90081736. E-mail：bympz@ycnzaegj.edu.cn

1368。火车站

广东省中山市振游路 438 号中山站（邮政编码：336445）。联系电话：32892730。电子邮箱：nlcfz@sqmvoxyk.chr.cn

Guǎngdōng Shěng Zhōngshān Shì Zhèn Yóu Lù 438 Hào Zōngsān Zhàn（Yóuzhèng Biānmǎ：336445). Liánxì Diànhuà：32892730. Diànzǐ Yóuxiāng：nlcfz@sqmvoxyk.chr.cn

Zhongshan Railway Station, 438 Zhen You Road, Zhongshan, Guangdong. Postal Code: 336445. Phone Number：32892730. E-mail：nlcfz@sqmvoxyk.chr.cn

1369。机场

广东省湛江市徐闻县昌屹路 432 号湛江亮惟国际机场（邮政编码：886288）。联系电话：51914707。电子邮箱：qbgas@slvhuqdb.airports.cn

Guǎngdōng Shěng Zhànjiāng Shì Xúwén Xiàn Chāng Yì Lù 432 Hào Zànjiāng Liàng Wéi Guó Jì Jī Chǎng（Yóuzhèng Biānmǎ：886288）. Liánxì Diànhuà：51914707. Diànzǐ Yóuxiāng：qbgas@slvhuqdb.airports.cn

Zhanjiang Liang Wei International Airport, 432 Chang Yi Road, Xuwen County, Zhanjiang, Guangdong. Postal Code: 886288. Phone Number：51914707. E-mail：qbgas@slvhuqdb.airports.cn

1370。家庭

广东省汕头市澄海区大食路 225 号进强公寓 29 层 533 室（邮政编码：382141）。联系电话：89191695。电子邮箱：pucfh@oyaqvcmj.cn

Guǎngdōng Shěng Shàntóu Shì Chénghǎi Qū Dài Sì Lù 225 Hào Jìn Qiǎng Gōng Yù 29 Céng 533 Shì (Yóuzhèng Biānmǎ：382141). Liánxì Diànhuà：89191695. Diànzǐ Yóuxiāng：pucfh@oyaqvcmj.cn

Room# 533, Floor# 29, Jin Qiang Apartment, 225 Dai Si Road, Chenghai District, Shantou, Guangdong. Postal Code: 382141. Phone Number：89191695. E-mail：pucfh@oyaqvcmj.cn

1371。公园

广东省潮州市饶平县甫可路 274 号光源公园（邮政编码：230785）。联系电话：36178422。电子邮箱：ohiyt@inqvdocy.parks.cn

Guǎngdōng Shěng Cháozhōu Shì Ráo Píng Xiàn Fǔ Kě Lù 274 Hào Guāng Yuán Gōng Yuán（Yóuzhèng Biānmǎ：230785). Liánxì Diànhuà：36178422. Diànzǐ Yóuxiāng：ohiyt@inqvdocy.parks.cn

Guang Yuan Park, 274 Fu Ke Road, Raoping County, Chaozhou, Guangdong. Postal Code: 230785. Phone Number：36178422. E-mail：ohiyt@inqvdocy.parks.cn

1372。湖泊

广东省珠海市金湾区亚毅路 361 号自先湖（ 邮政编码：677107）。联系电话：64456932。电子邮箱：dqtoy@uhnpzlvb.lakes.cn

Guǎngdōng Shěng Zhūhǎi Shì Jīn Wān Qū Yà Yì Lù 361 Hào Zì Xiān Hú （Yóuzhèng Biānmǎ：677107). Liánxì Diànhuà：64456932. Diànzǐ Yóuxiāng：dqtoy@uhnpzlvb.lakes.cn

Zi Xian Lake, 361 Ya Yi Road, Jinwan District, Zhuhai, Guangdong. Postal Code: 677107. Phone Number：64456932. E-mail：dqtoy@uhnpzlvb.lakes.cn

1373。酒店

广东省梅州市大埔县熔炯路 981 号圣歧酒店（ 邮政编码：176359）。联系电话：79860949。电子邮箱：czxwv@wksfvcxz.biz.cn

Guǎngdōng Shěng Méizhōu Shì Dà Bù Xiàn Róng Jiǒng Lù 981 Hào Shèng Qí Jiǔ Diàn （Yóuzhèng Biānmǎ：176359). Liánxì Diànhuà：79860949. Diànzǐ Yóuxiāng：czxwv@wksfvcxz.biz.cn

Sheng Qi Hotel, 981 Rong Jiong Road, Dapu County, Meizhou, Guangdong. Postal Code: 176359. Phone Number：79860949. E-mail：czxwv@wksfvcxz.biz.cn

1374。机场

广东省佛山市南海区白化路 965 号佛山兆祥国际机场（ 邮政编码：984455）。联系电话：19261829。电子邮箱：dqrjw@joxaipqz.airports.cn

Guǎngdōng Shěng Fúshān Shì Nánhǎi Qū Bái Huà Lù 965 Hào Fúsān Zhào Xiáng Guó Jì Jī Chǎng （Yóuzhèng Biānmǎ：984455). Liánxì Diànhuà：19261829. Diànzǐ Yóuxiāng：dqrjw@joxaipqz.airports.cn

Foshan Zhao Xiang International Airport, 965 Bai Hua Road, Nanhai District, Foshan, Guangdong. Postal Code: 984455. Phone Number：19261829. E-mail：dqrjw@joxaipqz.airports.cn

1375。公共汽车站

广东省肇庆市端州区稼大路 724 号可斌站（邮政编码：206389）。联系电话：42435986。电子邮箱：ckvqg@ftezlkyo.transport.cn

Guǎngdōng Shěng Zhàoqìng Shì Duān Zhōu Qū Jià Dà Lù 724 Hào Kě Bīn Zhàn (Yóuzhèng Biānmǎ：206389). Liánxì Diànhuà：42435986. Diànzǐ Yóuxiāng：ckvqg@ftezlkyo.transport.cn

Ke Bin Bus Station, 724 Jia Da Road, Duanzhou District, Zhaoqing, Guangdong. Postal Code: 206389. Phone Number：42435986. E-mail：ckvqg@ftezlkyo.transport.cn

1376。湖泊

广东省揭阳市揭西县石水路 783 号启舟湖（邮政编码：588708）。联系电话：70216944。电子邮箱：aglyx@xyawltge.lakes.cn

Guǎngdōng Shěng Jiēyáng Shì Jiē Xī Xiàn Dàn Shuǐ Lù 783 Hào Qǐ Zhōu Hú (Yóuzhèng Biānmǎ：588708). Liánxì Diànhuà：70216944. Diànzǐ Yóuxiāng：aglyx@xyawltge.lakes.cn

Qi Zhou Lake, 783 Dan Shui Road, Jiexi County, Jieyang, Guangdong. Postal Code: 588708. Phone Number：70216944. E-mail：aglyx@xyawltge.lakes.cn

1377。火车站

广东省茂名市高州市人冠路 512 号茂名站（邮政编码：495491）。联系电话：86019366。电子邮箱：xeyrb@pgzxeuts.chr.cn

Guǎngdōng Shěng Màomíng Shì Gāozhōu Shì Rén Guàn Lù 512 Hào Màomíng Zhàn（Yóuzhèng Biānmǎ：495491). Liánxì Diànhuà：86019366. Diànzǐ Yóuxiāng：xeyrb@pgzxeuts.chr.cn

Maoming Railway Station, 512 Ren Guan Road, Gaozhou, Maoming, Guangdong. Postal Code: 495491. Phone Number：86019366. E-mail：xeyrb@pgzxeuts.chr.cn

1378。公园

广东省阳江市江城区咚绅路 286 号翼刚公园（邮政编码：485880）。联系电话：11743599。电子邮箱：rketh@lqgihasc.parks.cn

Guǎngdōng Shěng Yángjiāng Shì Jiāng Chéngqū Dōng Shēn Lù 286 Hào Yì Gāng Gōng Yuán (Yóuzhèng Biānmǎ：485880). Liánxì Diànhuà：11743599. Diànzǐ Yóuxiāng：rketh@lqgihasc.parks.cn

Yi Gang Park, 286 Dong Shen Road, Jiangcheng District, Yangjiang, Guangdong. Postal Code: 485880. Phone Number：11743599. E-mail：rketh@lqgihasc.parks.cn

1379。酒店

广东省中山市秀寰路 629 号胜圣酒店（邮政编码：418613）。联系电话：24819616。电子邮箱：nhcgr@rfhatbgx.biz.cn

Guǎngdōng Shěng Zhōngshān Shì Xiù Huán Lù 629 Hào Shēng Shèng Jiǔ Diàn (Yóuzhèng Biānmǎ：418613). Liánxì Diànhuà：24819616. Diànzǐ Yóuxiāng：nhcgr@rfhatbgx.biz.cn

Sheng Sheng Hotel, 629 Xiu Huan Road, Zhongshan, Guangdong. Postal Code: 418613. Phone Number：24819616. E-mail：nhcgr@rfhatbgx.biz.cn

1380。大学

广东省江门市鹤山市己威大学可鸣路 754 号（邮政编码：316370）。联系电话：12222516。电子邮箱：emfrs@fthbyuks.edu.cn

Guǎngdōng Shěng Jiāngmén Shì Hèshān Shì Jǐ Wēi DàxuéKě Míng Lù 754 Hào (Yóuzhèng Biānmǎ：316370). Liánxì Diànhuà：12222516. Diànzǐ Yóuxiāng：emfrs@fthbyuks.edu.cn

Ji Wei University, 754 Ke Ming Road, Heshan City, Jiangmen, Guangdong. Postal Code: 316370. Phone Number：12222516. E-mail：emfrs@fthbyuks.edu.cn

CHAPTER 10: SENTENCES (181-200)

1381。公园

广东省江门市鹤山市鹤宽路 465 号化咚公园（邮政编码：790923）。联系电话：36904712。电子邮箱：gnflm@jmlqrgyo.parks.cn

Guǎngdōng Shěng Jiāngmén Shì Hèshān Shì Hè Kuān Lù 465 Hào Huā Dōng Gōng Yuán （Yóuzhèng Biānmǎ：790923). Liánxì Diànhuà：36904712. Diànzǐ Yóuxiāng：gnflm@jmlqrgyo.parks.cn

Hua Dong Park, 465 He Kuan Road, Heshan City, Jiangmen, Guangdong. Postal Code: 790923. Phone Number：36904712. E-mail：gnflm@jmlqrgyo.parks.cn

1382。家庭

广东省惠州市龙门县南泽路 574 号游风公寓 38 层 567 室（邮政编码：576356）。联系电话：30753579。电子邮箱：vkqne@epjsmfic.cn

Guǎngdōng Shěng Huìzhōu Shì Lóngmén Xiàn Nán Zé Lù 574 Hào Yóu Fēng Gōng Yù 38 Céng 567 Shì (Yóuzhèng Biānmǎ：576356). Liánxì Diànhuà：30753579. Diànzǐ Yóuxiāng：vkqne@epjsmfic.cn

Room# 567, Floor# 38, You Feng Apartment, 574 Nan Ze Road, Longmen County, Huizhou, Guangdong. Postal Code: 576356. Phone Number：30753579. E-mail：vkqne@epjsmfic.cn

1383。公共汽车站

广东省云浮市郁南县易源路 108 号维铁站（邮政编码：210175）。联系电话：92488266。电子邮箱：qsiml@xgfakqum.transport.cn

Guǎngdōng Shěng Yúnfú Shì Yù Nán Xiàn Yì Yuán Lù 108 Hào Wéi Fū Zhàn (Yóuzhèng Biānmǎ：210175). Liánxì Diànhuà：92488266. Diànzǐ Yóuxiāng：qsiml@xgfakqum.transport.cn

Wei Fu Bus Station, 108 Yi Yuan Road, Yunan County, Yunfu, Guangdong. Postal Code: 210175. Phone Number：92488266. E-mail：qsiml@xgfakqum.transport.cn

1384。广场

广东省湛江市麻章区乙星路 176 号中茂广场（邮政编码：720382）。联系电话：76105563。电子邮箱：shlnr@mukjshtx.squares.cn

Guǎngdōng Shěng Zhànjiāng Shì Má Zhāng Qū Yǐ Xīng Lù 176 Hào Zhōng Mào Guǎng Chǎng (Yóuzhèng Biānmǎ：720382). Liánxì Diànhuà：76105563. Diànzǐ Yóuxiāng：shlnr@mukjshtx.squares.cn

Zhong Mao Square, 176 Yi Xing Road, Machang District, Zhanjiang, Guangdong. Postal Code: 720382. Phone Number：76105563. E-mail：shlnr@mukjshtx.squares.cn

1385。湖泊

广东省揭阳市揭东区俊坡路 308 号彬仓湖（邮政编码：884236）。联系电话：23809978。电子邮箱：oevht@arpjlhot.lakes.cn

Guǎngdōng Shěng Jiēyáng Shì Jiē Dōngqū Jùn Pō Lù 308 Hào Bīn Cāng Hú (Yóuzhèng Biānmǎ：884236). Liánxì Diànhuà：23809978. Diànzǐ Yóuxiāng：oevht@arpjlhot.lakes.cn

Bin Cang Lake, 308 Jun Po Road, Jiedong District, Jieyang, Guangdong. Postal Code: 884236. Phone Number：23809978. E-mail：oevht@arpjlhot.lakes.cn

1386。火车站

广东省阳江市江城区轼大路 989 号阳江站（邮政编码：647588）。联系电话：66914089。电子邮箱：rxsyd@gjwoayvl.chr.cn

Guăngdōng Shěng Yángjiāng Shì Jiāng Chéngqū Shì Dà Lù 989 Hào Yángjiāng Zhàn (Yóuzhèng Biānmǎ：647588). Liánxì Diànhuà：66914089. Diànzǐ Yóuxiāng：rxsyd@gjwoayvl.chr.cn

Yangjiang Railway Station, 989 Shi Da Road, Jiangcheng District, Yangjiang, Guangdong. Postal Code: 647588. Phone Number：66914089. E-mail：rxsyd@gjwoayvl.chr.cn

1387。家庭

广东省湛江市坡头区福钢路 790 号屹臻公寓 1 层 259 室（邮政编码：796969）。联系电话：44230972。电子邮箱：ucosa@akdoylcr.cn

Guăngdōng Shěng Zhànjiāng Shì Pō Tóu Qū Fú Gāng Lù 790 Hào Yì Zhēn Gōng Yù 1 Céng 259 Shì (Yóuzhèng Biānmǎ：796969). Liánxì Diànhuà：44230972. Diànzǐ Yóuxiāng：ucosa@akdoylcr.cn

Room# 259, Floor# 1, Yi Zhen Apartment, 790 Fu Gang Road, Potou District, Zhanjiang, Guangdong. Postal Code: 796969. Phone Number：44230972. E-mail：ucosa@akdoylcr.cn

1388。公司

广东省韶关市曲江区陶风路 325 号庆德有限公司（邮政编码：779663）。联系电话：37539955。电子邮箱：qpuio@xeukatmp.biz.cn

Guăngdōng Shěng Sháoguān Shì Qū Jiāng Qū Táo Fēng Lù 325 Hào Qìng Dé Yǒuxiàn Gōngsī (Yóuzhèng Biānmǎ：779663). Liánxì Diànhuà：37539955. Diànzǐ Yóuxiāng：qpuio@xeukatmp.biz.cn

Qing De Corporation, 325 Tao Feng Road, Qujiang District, Shaoguan, Guangdong. Postal Code: 779663. Phone Number：37539955. E-mail：qpuio@xeukatmp.biz.cn

1389。大学

广东省东莞市斌风大学陶伦路 480 号（邮政编码：536810）。联系电话：91093428。电子邮箱：zbsyk@tghnflds.edu.cn

Guǎngdōng Shěng Dōngguǎn Shì Bīn Fēng DàxuéTáo Lún Lù 480 Hào （Yóuzhèng Biānmǎ：536810). Liánxì Diànhuà：91093428. Diànzǐ Yóuxiāng：zbsyk@tghnflds.edu.cn

Bin Feng University, 480 Tao Lun Road, Dongguan, Guangdong. Postal Code: 536810. Phone Number：91093428. E-mail：zbsyk@tghnflds.edu.cn

1390。酒店

广东省揭阳市普宁市陆己路 288 号惟冕酒店（邮政编码：184227）。联系电话：87732595。电子邮箱：mkzgi@pimoabdx.biz.cn

Guǎngdōng Shěng Jiēyáng Shì Pǔníng Shì Lù Jǐ Lù 288 Hào Wéi Miǎn Jiǔ Diàn （Yóuzhèng Biānmǎ：184227). Liánxì Diànhuà：87732595. Diànzǐ Yóuxiāng：mkzgi@pimoabdx.biz.cn

Wei Mian Hotel, 288 Lu Ji Road, Puning City, Jieyang, Guangdong. Postal Code: 184227. Phone Number：87732595. E-mail：mkzgi@pimoabdx.biz.cn

1391。湖泊

广东省汕头市金平区桥翰路 640 号金汉湖（邮政编码：656381）。联系电话：14130067。电子邮箱：xfplw@bqslhgwo.lakes.cn

Guǎngdōng Shěng Shàntóu Shì Jīnpíng Qū Qiáo Hàn Lù 640 Hào Jīn Hàn Hú （Yóuzhèng Biānmǎ：656381). Liánxì Diànhuà：14130067. Diànzǐ Yóuxiāng：xfplw@bqslhgwo.lakes.cn

Jin Han Lake, 640 Qiao Han Road, Jinping District, Shantou, Guangdong. Postal Code: 656381. Phone Number：14130067. E-mail：xfplw@bqslhgwo.lakes.cn

1392。博物院

广东省湛江市麻章区强领路 131 号湛江博物馆（邮政编码：405861）。联系电话：97186284。电子邮箱：wntsf@ykcvbxpd.museums.cn

Guǎngdōng Shěng Zhànjiāng Shì Má Zhāng Qū Qiáng Lǐng Lù 131 Hào Zànjiāng Bó Wù Guǎn（Yóuzhèng Biānmǎ：405861). Liánxì Diànhuà：97186284. Diànzǐ Yóuxiāng：wntsf@ykcvbxpd.museums.cn

Zhanjiang Museum, 131 Qiang Ling Road, Machang District, Zhanjiang, Guangdong. Postal Code: 405861. Phone Number：97186284. E-mail：wntsf@ykcvbxpd.museums.cn

1393。公司

广东省河源市和平县仲化路 457 号钊舟有限公司（邮政编码：904859）。联系电话：44054911。电子邮箱：rcweb@epdtsurv.biz.cn

Guǎngdōng Shěng Héyuán Shì Hépíng Xiàn Zhòng Huà Lù 457 Hào Zhāo Zhōu Yǒuxiàn Gōngsī（Yóuzhèng Biānmǎ：904859). Liánxì Diànhuà：44054911. Diànzǐ Yóuxiāng：rcweb@epdtsurv.biz.cn

Zhao Zhou Corporation, 457 Zhong Hua Road, Heping County, Heyuan, Guangdong. Postal Code: 904859. Phone Number：44054911. E-mail：rcweb@epdtsurv.biz.cn

1394。公园

广东省肇庆市广宁县尚晖路 339 号岐晖公园（邮政编码：162643）。联系电话：34877317。电子邮箱：jqrgw@yedshqrf.parks.cn

Guǎngdōng Shěng Zhàoqìng Shì Guǎng Níngxiàn Shàng Huī Lù 339 Hào Qí Huī Gōng Yuán（Yóuzhèng Biānmǎ：162643). Liánxì Diànhuà：34877317. Diànzǐ Yóuxiāng：jqrgw@yedshqrf.parks.cn

Qi Hui Park, 339 Shang Hui Road, Guangning County, Zhaoqing, Guangdong. Postal Code: 162643. Phone Number：34877317. E-mail：jqrgw@yedshqrf.parks.cn

1395。机场

广东省茂名市茂南区食稼路 855 号茂名葛光国际机场（ 邮政编码：179119）。联系电话：90474651。电子邮箱：xirlk@nxarvkdu.airports.cn

Guǎngdōng Shěng Màomíng Shì Mào Nán Qū Yì Jià Lù 855 Hào Màomíng Gé Guāng Guó Jì Jī Chǎng (Yóuzhèng Biānmǎ：179119). Liánxì Diànhuà：90474651. Diànzǐ Yóuxiāng：xirlk@nxarvkdu.airports.cn

Maoming Ge Guang International Airport, 855 Yi Jia Road, Maonan District, Maoming, Guangdong. Postal Code: 179119. Phone Number：90474651. E-mail：xirlk@nxarvkdu.airports.cn

1396。家庭

广东省梅州市丰顺县际茂路 375 号泽超公寓 13 层 196 室（ 邮政编码：433357）。联系电话：26394652。电子邮箱：rjlxg@adtgcrpl.cn

Guǎngdōng Shěng Méizhōu Shì Fēng Shùn Xiàn Jì Mào Lù 375 Hào Zé Chāo Gōng Yù 13 Céng 196 Shì (Yóuzhèng Biānmǎ：433357). Liánxì Diànhuà：26394652. Diànzǐ Yóuxiāng：rjlxg@adtgcrpl.cn

Room# 196, Floor# 13, Ze Chao Apartment, 375 Ji Mao Road, Fengshun County, Meizhou, Guangdong. Postal Code: 433357. Phone Number：26394652. E-mail：rjlxg@adtgcrpl.cn

1397。酒店

广东省珠海市香洲区来坡路 737 号易毅酒店（ 邮政编码：789716）。联系电话：91850303。电子邮箱：nqrfu@wfcnziak.biz.cn

Guǎngdōng Shěng Zhūhǎi Shì Xiāngzhōu Qū Lái Pō Lù 737 Hào Yì Yì Jiǔ Diàn (Yóuzhèng Biānmǎ：789716). Liánxì Diànhuà：91850303. Diànzǐ Yóuxiāng：nqrfu@wfcnziak.biz.cn

Yi Yi Hotel, 737 Lai Po Road, Xiangzhou District, Zhuhai, Guangdong. Postal Code: 789716. Phone Number：91850303. E-mail：nqrfu@wfcnziak.biz.cn

1398。广场

广东省广州市海珠区亚不路 274 号振浩广场（邮政编码：465636）。联系电话：98103124。电子邮箱：melgt@zlkfuxep.squares.cn

Guǎngdōng Shěng Guǎngzhōu Shì Hǎizhū Qū Yà Bù Lù 274 Hào Zhèn Hào Guǎng Chǎng （Yóuzhèng Biānmǎ：465636). Liánxì Diànhuà：98103124. Diànzǐ Yóuxiāng：melgt@zlkfuxep.squares.cn

Zhen Hao Square, 274 Ya Bu Road, Haizhu District, Guangzhou, Guangdong. Postal Code: 465636. Phone Number：98103124. E-mail：melgt@zlkfuxep.squares.cn

1399。公共汽车站

广东省梅州市平远县奎原路 491 号星屹站（邮政编码：248173）。联系电话：37823722。电子邮箱：acymk@lcqhjgps.transport.cn

Guǎngdōng Shěng Méizhōu Shì Píng Yuǎn Xiàn Kuí Yuán Lù 491 Hào Xīng Yì Zhàn （Yóuzhèng Biānmǎ：248173). Liánxì Diànhuà：37823722. Diànzǐ Yóuxiāng：acymk@lcqhjgps.transport.cn

Xing Yi Bus Station, 491 Kui Yuan Road, Pingyuan County, Meizhou, Guangdong. Postal Code: 248173. Phone Number：37823722. E-mail：acymk@lcqhjgps.transport.cn

1400。医院

广东省汕尾市陆河县阳骥路 226 号轼淹医院（邮政编码：213464）。联系电话：75278269。电子邮箱：lozkj@kxnvwpcb.health.cn

Guǎngdōng Shěng Shànwěi Shì Lù Hé Xiàn Yáng Jì Lù 226 Hào Shì Yān Yī Yuàn （Yóuzhèng Biānmǎ：213464). Liánxì Diànhuà：75278269. Diànzǐ Yóuxiāng：lozkj@kxnvwpcb.health.cn

Shi Yan Hospital, 226 Yang Ji Road, Luhe County, Shanwei, Guangdong. Postal Code: 213464. Phone Number：75278269. E-mail：lozkj@kxnvwpcb.health.cn